COPY©PROOF
A New Method for Design and Education
POST ST. JOOST
Edited by
Edith Gruson & Gert Staal

010 Publishers, Rotterdam 2000

·2012·

COPY®PROOF
Graphic Design
as Visual Rhetoric
Principles for
Design Education
HUGUES C. BOEKRAAD

The Impossibility of Teaching Design Design education has never stood on very solid ground, but today it seems to be floating on particularly precarious shifting sands. There are designers employed as teachers who even feel that teaching design is in principle an impossibility, because the field of design moves too quickly and develops in so many directions at once. Such an appeal to the rapid tempo of innovation in design, is not however, a convincing argument. A comparison with other fast-developing disciplines – consider information technology or bio-technology – makes this immediately clear. The source of the very real dilemma in design education lies elsewhere. What is missing is a more or less consistent theory about what design actually is. Equally, for those actively practicing in the many professional areas that the term 'design' entails, it is in fact unclear what this term exactly means.

Design is a heuristic technique. Heuristic techniques are familiar to science, but the overlap does not make design a scientific discipline. Design, for example, has no isolated object for research. Design is a project, not an object. The lawyer, the economist, the sociologist, all research the world in its respective legal, economic or sociological aspects. But under which aspect does the designer investigate the world? Is the artificiality of the world his object? This view, put forward by Herbert Simon, is defensible, but it does make the designer's domain an unnavigable one, and does not make its invention a science.

Designing is moreover not a craft, which would be defined as a capability in terms of fixed, prescribed tasks, materials and forms. Although the elements and skills of craftsmanship are part of design, design is without its fixed, prescribed elements. Design, after all, involves the application of new materials, thinking up new forms and carrying out new types of tasks.

Finally, designing is not one of the autonomous fine arts. It cannot be reduced to aesthetics, and the impulse for a design comes from an outside source, from the client. Designing is a social activity. The problem of teaching design is consequently in part created by the inability to define the activity of designing, and from the hybrid definitions on which designers and design educators rely. Where there is no design theory at hand, it should not be surprising that there is no consistent design pedagogy.

There are means, some more elegant than others, by which the designer delivers himself from this impasse. The most common is an anti-intellectual approach: the question of what design is, is not relevant for the designer. Designing is an ability, a savoir faire. It is very possible to make something without first asking yourself what that 'making' is. Worse, asking yourself what it is even gets in the way of an optimal process. In the eyes of this genre of designers, a theory is not only superfluous but even harmful.

Rather than seeking a foundation in theory, design training clings to dominant styles or schools of design. This education then imparts the knowledge, the procedures, the skills and the attitudes of the selected example, so that students learn to design in the style of such a school. (This is one of the reasons why modernism has become a style.) Imitating a style or a design method would hardly seem to qualify as an ideal preparation for professional designing, and it is in fact a contradiction of what designing essentially is.

Another way of getting out of the theoretical discomfiture is rather more complicated. Designing is localized in the margins of other, more stable practices. Designing now becomes defined as a melange of art, science and technology. This was the solution to the impasse opted for by the twentieth century's most famous schools of design, the Bauhaus in Weimar, Dessau and Berlin (1919-1933), the New Bauhaus in Chicago (1937-1955) and the Hochschule für Gestaltung in Ulm (1953-1968). All three saw the fusion of art, technology and science as the core of design and of design education. The problem of this solution is indeed that design is defined in terms of disciplines whose foundations are essentially different from those of design.

Why is there no General Theory of Design? What makes it so difficult to get a grip on the various design disciplines? There are several factors we can point to. In the first place are the historic origins of the profession in the crafts and trades. Designing at that point concerned material objects that were designed and produced by the same person. Designing something and making it were mutual extensions of one another, and for this reason did not have to be conceptually distinct. Since then, industrial production has certainly put an end to this fusion of design and production that once characterized the craftsman's production methods. Products are now manufactured in the framework of a technological and economic system in which design itself has become a specialized activity. This specialization is expressed in the realization of a prototype or model. The model is indeed often made with traditional craftsman's techniques, so that its designer might still picture himself as designer and maker, without really differentiating the two.

He would, however, be denying the fact that the invention and construction of that model is taking place within a system of different disciplines, all of which help determine the outer appearance of the product. When the designer wants to be aware of his own personal contribution to the invention of that model, as well as of the external influences on his design, he will have to be capable of some degree of theoretical reflection.

Secondly, in the latter half of the nineteenth century, as a number of design proto-professions were developing, their practitioners were recruited from the ranks of architects and artists. Their self-image, their professional principles, as well as the concepts, terminology and notions that they used in their professional discourse, functioned as a screen, obscuring the design process itself. The designer's initial, uncertain status resulted in his preferring to define himself in terms of established artistic practices. Design was unjustly seen as industrial art, functional art or applied art.

The third factor that presents an obstacle to design theory is that design has long since ceased to concern exclusively material objects. Richard Buchanan distinguishes four categories of design: the design of symbolic and visual communication, the design of material objects, the design of activities and services, and the design of complex systems or environments for domestic life, work, play or learning. These distinct design activities certainly do not always result in material objects, but they do always result in models. Buchanan's divisions in types of design moreover make it clear how complex even the design of material objects has become. Influenced by the communications paradigm that, since World War II, has fundamentally changed both the individual and the image of society in the West, producers and consumers have continually gained more insight into the communicative dimension, including that of objects. It is expected of the designer that he or she be capable of applying rhetorical and semantic knowledge, aimed at the communicative context in which the design is to be used or experienced. But not only that. The designer must moreover be aware that the communicative context of his or her design will subsequently function in the framework of larger systems, cycles and environments. The boundaries dividing the diverse design disciplines are becoming indistinct, not simply because they are all making use of the same tool – the computer – as some people claim, but because the social systems in and for which designs are made are forcing the integration of the competencies of previously different disciplines. This is the fourth factor that stands in the way of a theory of design.

Finally, in what context is such a theory to be developed? Design practice, design education, design criticism and academic research into design are the obvious and appropriate places, but we have to conclude that for differing reasons, they have as yet produced insufficient results.

Graphic Design as Symbolic and Visual Communication: Successive Paradigms   We will limit ourselves here to one of the design categories distinguished by Buchanan: symbolic and visual communication. To identify the specific theoretical problems here, and the paradigms that have developed over the course of time, we first provide a brief outline of what it entails. The general title under which the symbolic and visual designer operates is that of graphic designer. The term dates back to the time when professional communications took place via the products of graphics technology and the printing industry. The profession of graphic designer arose as part of the activities of printing and publishing houses, in the context of providing different printed forms and typography. The first definition of graphic design was putting text into typographic form. The graphic designer's medium was the book.

In the second half of the nineteenth century, graphic design was redefined, and in two opposing forms. The first acclaimed technological innovation, with the invention of colour lithography. On returning to Paris from London 1866, Jules Chéret (1836-1932) produced an extensive oeuvre of graphic work, colour lithograph posters printed separately for each colour and in multiple editions, which were simultaneously distributed throughout the urban environment. Chéret, in effect the inventor of a new form of communication, saw himself as a graphic artist. Eventually, around 1900, he was recognized as such in the art world. The text in his work was integrated into a visual image.

The second redefinition in fact resisted innovations in graphics technology. The Arts and Crafts Movement returned to the traditional techniques of manufacturing books, also employing them for such products as wallpaper, tapestries, and so on. As had Chéret, William Morris (1834-1896) brought text into the framework of an expressive and/or decorative design. In this case, graphic design was now a form of monumental art or craft. Text was decorated.

Modernism, in its own turn, rejected both the anti-technological standpoints of the Arts and Crafts Movement and the expressive dimension of the functional arts. In late modernism, finally, graphic design was perceived as an ordering of information. Text had by now become encoded in a typographic grid system. In short, this system typography amounted to standardizing the application of graphics variables. For as far as there was a theory behind it, this was borrowed from communications theory and focussed on the sign, not on the image. Representation was stripped of its political and social implications and reduced to information. Diverse design questions were dealt with according to a single method, one which did not derive from the given theme or the particular commissioned task. The aesthetic side of the design, its atmosphere and beauty, were covertly taken into account, but officially, they were taboo. Finally, communicative design was equally defrauded of its rhetorical dimension. The reader or observer did not need to be convinced of anything or emotionally affected, but merely informed.

Towards the end of the 1970s, late modernism had expended itself. Not only its language of form was under debate, but so was its methodology. While the late modernists adhered to a definition of design as problem-solving and as an organization of information, since the 1980s, design has primarily been seen as fun, as the creation of a pleasing visual environment. This change of paradigm was introduced by alterations in communications strategies, which were in turn brought on by social and technological changes. Late modernism took for granted a universal and rational recipient for its message. In postmodernism, there is no longer any place for such an assumption. Communications target groups are divided into niches and segments, their differences articulated in terms of age, class, gender or ethnic group. Graphic design is increasingly involved in market-oriented activities.

The introduction of the computer, which – since the 1980s – has had a direct influence on changing the symbolic and visual communications paradigm, brought with it acute problems for design education. Many teachers lacked expertise in the new information technology and suddenly found themselves virtually incompetent, at least as long as we assume that teachers train students in the design tasks of tomorrow, not those of yesterday. Add to this the fact that the computer is not only a completely different design medium – moving images and sound were not part of the traditional graphic designer's tool kit – but it has moreover created an entirely new communications environment. Meanwhile, about 15% of production in Dutch graphic design studios is for the new media. Even more significant a factor is the rapid pace at which new studios, with designers fresh out of school, are specializing in the new fields. To date, young teachers who do have command of the required expertise often miss the reflexive distance required, for example, to set quality criteria and to formulate an aesthetic.

Method as a Principle for Design Education   Surveying the design field in general, and graphic design in particular, there are three approaches that present themselves for a pedagogy of graphic design.

Open the academy doors wide, permitting entry for current practice. In doing so, however, keep in mind that practices are very diverse and for that reason cannot in themselves provide a didactic model or a coherent curriculum. Which designers should be invited to teach and why?

Make the programme less teacher-dependent and streamline it by means of modules. Transform the teacher into a coach and encourage students to work independently according to the learning-to-learn model. In practice, we see that this model is enjoying increasing attention, in particular from the management of educational institutions and from the government bodies that support them.

Create the time and the space for reflection on the profession, and particularly on theory. What are the social foundations supporting the various design practices, and if such a social foundation exists, can it serve as the basis for a professional pedagogy? What are the relevant disciplines in the social and cultural sciences that can help the practising designer? Here too, we already see that the first steps are being taken out in the field. Theoretical interest is on the rise, in design journals and seminars as well as in workshops for professional designers. Since the 1980s, semiotics, the history of graphic design, philosophy and communications theory have all won themselves a place in design education.

These strategies to resolve the 'unteachability' of design nonetheless still bypass the core of the problem. There is still the need for an elementary consensus concerning the nature of communicative design under the new cultural and technological conditions. From there, a consensus should directly follow on the methods by which a future designer achieves competence. Learning design methods and acquiring the capacity to vary these methods and allow them to evolve, is at the heart of design education. Education in design must therefore liberate itself from specific objects, styles and media. In their place, the focus should be on the design method itself, which as we have seen, consists of the design and creation of models. How do we now arrive at a model for communications? In order to do this, the designer requires knowledge and skills in generating, applying and manipulating signs, images and symbols. But most of all, his or her heuristic techniques must be developed, methods of inventing form. Insight into and controlled variation of the design process frees the designer, on the one hand, from a rigid, schematic approach, and on the other, from the uncontrollability of, the impulsive, one-of-a-kind discovery he is incapable of repeating. This process is not a solo activity of the designer sequestered off in his studio. The designer operates under procedural, technological, organizational and financial conditions. At a variety of crucial points in this design process, there is interaction with the client. How does the designer interpret that client's strategic objectives and ideas? How does he or she put them into his or her own ideas, words and images? And how does he present his ideas and forms?

An adequate design method is the only thing that offers an escape from this labyrinth of possibilities and choices. Finding that escape cannot be learned in a learning-to-learn didactic, nor by raiding information from the internet or by discussions with other students. The primary requirement is a reflection on method, as well as a willingness to be receptive to a reorientation to design. Current education in design puts too much emphasis on results and too little on the method of achieving them. This method must be based on a model – however schematic – of professional communications practice.

The Two Axes of Communicative Design   To examine professional communications, the practice of graphic design is a complex combination of two types of activities, the one communicative and the other aesthetic. The aesthetic activity of the graphic designer is comprised of giving form to the text provided by the client. He rearranges a text into an image. A writer's copy is translated by the book typographer into page form, the appearance of a text. In posters or billboards, text and image are mutually integrated, and in the magazine, the same thing happens in a sequence of spreads. This translation is not a slavish translation, but a creative interpretation that plays on both the visual registers and the textual registers at the same time, with the standard or quality of the designer primarily being judged on aesthetic criteria.

At the same time, the designer takes on an entirely different activity. What he is designing is a medium for communication between his client and that client's public. The selection of the target group and the tone and means with which that group is spoken to depends on the client, who wants to realize a communications strategy by means of the design. The most important criteria used by the client to judge the design is its effectiveness.

These two activities certainly intersect. Each influences the other and determines the conditions for the other. The style that the designer chooses is directly related to the means with which the client wishes to reach his public. I have previously described this as follows: The way the client perceives and defines his public determines the means which the designer will use to shape the text he designs.

We can now schematically represent the design process with two intersecting axes. The horizontal axis represents the activities of inventing images and designing forms. This is the aesthetic axis. The vertical axis represents the medium that communicates between the client and the public. It is the strategic communications axis.

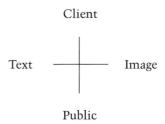

It has proven to be difficult to deal with both aspects in a single integrated theory. There is also something about design practice itself that resists this, ensconced in the designer's desire to maintain his own autonomy in relation to his client. The aesthetic axis then represents the domain of his artistic freedom. The communications axis is seen as that of external determinants – a restriction of his freedom of action. The fact that design education is overwhelmingly incorporated into art schools and academies has largely contributed to autonomy being perceived as the key to the self-image of future designers and to the ideology of their education. Design hereby becomes a specific variant of the fine arts. In the first four years of design school, communications is an isolated context which in almost all cases is summarily pushed out of the way. In student assignments – except for some classes in theory, design education consists almost exclusively of problem-solving exercises – the entire emphasis falls on the relationship between the form and what it means, which is to say, the translation of text into image. Practical, professional experience is dealt with in the form of an external practice apprenticeship (internship). Consequently, the communicative realities of the design process are projected outside of the academy.

To return to the problem of combining both axes, Richard Buchanan, Gui Bonsiepe, Robin Kinross and Hanno Ehses have all spoken of graphic design as a form of visual rhetoric. But as far as I know, they have not yet adopted this visual rhetoric as a matrix for setting up a new type of exercise or assignment in design education. For them, rhetoric is purely an element of the theory of design. Since 1995, one thing that has specifically characterized a graduate education in design at the St. Joost Academy in Breda is the mutual integration of theory and practical exercises. During the first four years of the Post-St. Joost programme, designer Gerard Hadders, Edith Gruson, and myself (familiar with design practice not as a designer, but as the client) have not only designed exercises together, but have also collaborated in guiding and evaluating their progress. In 1996, we introduced the visual essay as a design method, with the visual rhetoric as leitmotif.

Visual Rhetoric   Perhaps it would not be superfluous to indicate here what rhetoric actually is. In everyday speech, the words 'rhetoric' and 'rhetorical' are often used in a pejorative sense, usually implying a demagogic use of language meant to manipulate others, to disguise the real feelings or meaning of the speaker and/or distort reality. Rhetorical language consequently lies close to untruth and misleading. In the worst case, it is about lies. In all cases, it concerns interests and speaking from the perspective of those interests. Rhetoric, as a consequence, is the opposite of clear, transparent communication, which is supposed to be free of interests and limited solely to facts and data.

An entirely different history of rhetoric contrasts with this common perception, as does a true renaissance of rhetoric that has been taking place since the 1970s. Rhetoric is the art of speaking and writing well on any and all matters that fall outside pure science or technique. In short, rhetoric is the vehicle of practical reasoning, or to quote the 18th-century Neapolitan cultural theorist, Giovanni Battista Vico, 'What is eloquence if not wisdom expressed in an elegant manner, richly flowered and in accordance with healthy reasoning?'

Rhetoric is one of the liberal arts, which is to say, an art that must be mastered by the free man. As opposed to science, which tries to formulate true statements, rhetoric is available to formulate probable statements about matters of human concern. For centuries, rhetoric has taught the elite of the nations of Europe to speak in public, whether it be from the pulpit, the university podium, in the courtroom, in political meetings from the speaker's chair or the public tribune. Rhetoric was the vehicle of public opinion. Here lies a connection with graphic design that indeed cannot be dismissed from the public sphere as it developed after the seventeenth century. At the end of the nineteenth century, rhetoric was removed as a subject in secondary education, to be replaced by verbal comprehension or text interpretation. For the proponents of radical, mass democracy, rhetoric had become associated with the exercise of power by the old elite, and was consequently condemned. The abolition of verbal rhetoric as a means of forming the managerial, political, legal, scientific and religious elite came hand in hand with the discovery of visual rhetoric as a means of mass communication. This took form in the posters produced by Jules Chéret and his contemporaries. Rhetoric is at this point no longer perceived as the art of speech, but as a strategic simulation, and the return of the rhetoric of spoken text in the medium of reproduced text. Graphic design, just as classical rhetoric, is about reducing or eliminating the distance between the sender of the text and the recipient. Design is thereby a rhetorical practice of the second degree, an ability, a savoir faire indeed, but also a theory of that ability, as is classical rhetoric.

The teaching of rhetoric comprises five central elements that are also central elements of visual communications. These elements are the *inventio*, the *disposito*, the *elocutio*, the *memoria* and the *actio*. In graphic design, the retention and declamation of the text are replaced by mechanical or electronic reproduction. The inventio, disposito and elocutio remain in full force as part of the designer's package of tasks.

The inventio is the thinking up of an idea or ideas that one wishes to spotlight. In this context, relevant material is selected that will illustrate the subject and reinforce the concept or statement. The dispositio is the composition of the arguments. These must be arranged into an effective whole. The elocutio concerns the verbalization of the thought, the packaging or adorning of the arguments conceived. This is the stylistic refinement of the argument. It must be coordinated to suit the threshold of public expectation, but at the same time seduce and surprise that public. The arguments must be understandable and clear, visualized and verbalized correctly and effectively, and presented with a decorum appropriate to the circumstances. Hanno Ehses succumbs to the trap of aesthetic reduction of the design process by suggesting that it is primarily the elocution – stylistic skill – that is most important to the designer. In contrast, I would propose that (visual) communications is a more or less creative manipulation of commonalities – whether out of date or otherwise. The topica, therefore – the doctrine of commonplace – is at least as essential to any designer who knows that effective communication depends on that tiny twist applied to the familiar cliché.

The idea of graphic design as a rhetorical practice also makes it possible to rethink the different paradigms of the history of design. Looking first at the inventio, classic book typography made use of the compositional codes of previous generations of printers and typographers, albeit that the arrangement of text went hand in hand with additional ornamentation. Inventing form used to be limited to thinking up rules for standardization. In the postmodern context, in contrast, this orderly arrangement is not infrequently overrun by illustrative elements in which invention has free rein, creating style that can be all but impossible to follow. Stylistic complexity and an excessive desire for decoration are characteristic of postmodern design, at the expense of effective argumentation and composition. In the context of this publication, this argument is limited to a number of fundamental principles for education in (graphic) design. A detailed description of a curriculum structure or a design method, such as the visual essay, would be superfluous here, and the essay by Gert Staal, as well as the contributions of the (graduated) students, give a fair indication of their nature. What would be of value here is a comment about the relationship between visual rhetoric and the visual essay. The point of departure of the visual essay is not theory, but practice. As an educational instrument, it carries forward and builds on what graphic designers have themselves come up with in the practice of their profession. The visual essay has furthermore had an important and extremely interesting background in the history of visual communications, one which I hope to discuss at another opportunity.

In the framework of design education, what this concerns is the visual essay taking (back) a design method and a design genre from professional practice, in order to apply it to the pedagogy of the profession. The visual essay – along with its specific theme – always deals with insight into the way the designer sets to work in order to arrive at the form of his proposal, making the proposal convincing. The visual essay brings the visual arguments and the working methods of the designer into view, thereby providing the designer with grounds to be on equal footing with the client. Its persuasive character is familiar to the client, who is thinking in terms of strategic communications. But at the same time, for the designer, it defines the field of his own competence: the capacity to think in images. The demarcation that separates his advance research and his finding the solution is eliminated, as the visual essay embraces a report of this research. The visual essay not only shows the beginning of the design investigation (the intuitive trouvaille) or the final proposal for the form (the design), but a reconstructed version of the route in between the two: the method. With it, the designer wins the free, equal status that the late modernist in his day likewise attributed to the superiority of his method. The only difference is that the method has since been drastically changed.

i
we
they

i
identities

we
public sphere and urban space

they
proposal > < counter-proposal

Is an art school, by definition, destined to educate and train its students according to a model set by the professional practices of an earlier decade? Or perhaps even a stage earlier, dating from the time when the teachers themselves were educated? That would be twenty, sometimes thirty years before, conforming

to standards their own instructors adopted when (and now we are back to the early 20th century) they themselves chose to train in the profession of professions. In this case, this is graphic design, newly evolving from another form of graphic design, and just a generation before that the craft of typography and printmaking. Before you know it you are back in the arms of Paul Schuitema and Piet Zwart. The ideology of the New Art School would still be the norm for students of a profession that, under the influence of all sorts of social, economic and technological factors, has as much in common with the professional skills that gave rise to the PTT Book or the Syst-o-Color colour systems of the 1910s and 1930s as it has with the painting in the Sistine Chapel.

Designing in Complexity – the Fundamentals Post-St. Joost, the second or graduate phase of training offered at the St. Joost Academy in Breda, has been well aware of this dilemma since its inception in 1995. Designing today owes much of its legitimacy and practical content to the traditions of classic book typography, and it is certainly indebted to the inventiveness of the New Typographers and their followers, but it must also measure itself by the new mores of the communications and networking society. With iron-clad paradigms, these mores force us into greater and greater specialization, at the same time that the applicability of these specializations are continually being subjected to change. The medium or product is much more susceptible to change than the methods employed by their designer, and for this reason, Post-St.Joost does not offer a medium-specific education, but instead attempts to introduce a methodology that is both resistant to and open to technological, economic and cultural innovation.

At the start of the new millennium, the effects of the information age are no longer a futuristic fantasy, but a reality in which clients and designers must adapt their practices of thought and behaviour, just as the users of their products are having to do. Styles have become more multifarious. Information is disseminated by one new medium after another and must be designed for the characteristics of those media, and the distinct division between commercial and non-commercial communication has faded. Our discipline has consequently been released from a long heritage of sanctimoniousness – almost no one takes the myth of the designer as an autonomous, indeed even genius, problem-solver seriously any more – but it must learn a new language. That language has to respond to the understanding of parties which until recently could easily be dismissed as a credulous 'other' world: the blind in the land of the Cyclops.

The reality of the communications world has meanwhile become too hybrid for such categorical self-satisfaction. Its direction lies in new hands. The designer genius will be as incapable of determining the identity of a company as a gardener is of rearranging the topography of the whole park. Equally, design has become a profession that can no longer seek its challenges in time-honoured practices or techniques. That job can now be completed by clever software or inexpensive computer slaves.

In a scala of varying roles, graphic designers can be involved, for example, in realizing a corporate identity, but they will never again – as in the heyday of such studios as Pentagram and Total Design – be the intellectual owners of the whole process. Many parties are involved in steering the processes of image development, which are growing more and more complex, and the designer is a part of that community. Each link is judged according to its own merits and is as indispensable as it is powerless, the designers who come up with the concepts no less than the computer champions.

Three themes determine the curriculum of the graduate programme at Post-St. Joost: identities; urban space and accessibility; and proposal and counter-proposal. The themes are interrelated and in fact extend their reach, step by step. From the complexity of the person of the designer himself, the perspective shifts to that of the city and on to the design situation. I – we – they: this is the substance of the two-year graduate programme library.

Identities and Contexts - Themes With these themes, a design method is introduced, one which is not specifically tailored for academic courses at an art school. Thinking in terms of models, which forms the method's foundation, has proven applicable to both the educational situation and in professional practice. It embraces a logically planned, process-orientated and focussed resolution of design problems that, from the moment of the initial briefing, can never again be seen as simple linear problems. Time and again, by way of investigation, analysis, presentation, alternative scenarios and checks and balances from both sides, the designer and the 'client' – in this case the one providing the design assignment – modify their concepts until the definitive design can be

Retelling

'Being able to look analytically at problems in their context and especially at the connections between them, wanting to retell a story, not because you like retelling it so much, but because there is an ultimately valid reason for a new interpretation: this is what we ask. At the same time, you must be capable of reflecting on the methods of your own actions. In this process, arguments related to taste and personal preference are quickly killed off. You learn how to eliminate.'
Interview with Edith Gruson, 4 November, 1999

'Many of the tales told in our students' projects are about the impossibility of the telling, about the complexity of the different registrations of language and image, about lack of understanding between cultures. This work often takes place at the crossroads between the possible and the impossible, at the boundary of two worlds.'
Interview with Hugues Boekraad, 4 November, 1999

produced. Sound theoretical contexts, as well as insights and perceptions from the 'outside' world, provide added direction and guidance.

It is no accident that guest instructors from the world of forensic
research, poetry, archaeology, the media or, for example, the
museums, are closely involved in the realization of the projects. It
is also for this same reason that the essays in the second section of
this publication are written by people outside the field of graphic
design. Designing for fellow designers may well lead to a celebrated
career in the bosom of the minute in-crowd of the graphics world,
but it is not the approach chosen by Post-St. Joost.

IDENTITIES
Theme I
Forensic Self Portrait
& Imaginary Portrait

Three Squares

Post-St. Joost has set itself the goal of training designers capable of bringing a personal and professional identity to our environment, an approach that makes them capable of assuming a relevant position in the communications process. This relevance is not only in terms of one's own principles or the expectations of the client, but it is also in respect to the society in which the work has to function. After all, graphic designers construct images for the products made by their clients, and to a greater or lesser degree, make it possible for third parties to identify with those products. But what is the identity of the designer?

In the classic view of the romantic artist, the personality of the artist – and accordingly, of the designer – is seen as the primary source of the work. This is an intolerable assumption for a designer, if only because their work is not solely the reflection of a person, but equally that of the assignment and of the one who ultimately sees it. Nonetheless, in undergraduate design education, the design process is still often focussed on the personality cult. The development of the individual 'handwriting' is still the ultimate goal.

A Forensic and an Imaginary Portrait Post-St.Joost in fact begins with a dismantling of the acquired role of the designer. By having students come up with a so-called forensic self-portrait, and then an imaginary portrait, the process of 'deconstructing the designer' is begun. It is not the familiar repertoire of fonts, images, colour and layout that must tell the tale, but ordinary, everyday intimacies. The forensic 'proof' is arranged on a two-metre square 'canvas', sketching an image of the maker which must in turn be read and identified by outside parties, in this case the other students. They are the detectives who have to reconstruct an identity on the basis of the available clues. Those providing the clues have written down in advance how they think they will be perceived, but will the story be interpreted the way they expected? How great is the gap between intent and interpretation?

The forensic self-portrait and the imaginary portrait, in which a fictional personality is sketched with similar means, touch the very core of the graphic design profession. They raise questions about how we decipher the signs and characters that serve as glossaries, symbols or icons. They demonstrate how every communication is subject to several interpretations and that the designer is able to manipulate that perception when he is capable of making the leap between his own perceptions and those of the viewer. These 'outside views' are represented by several visiting lecturers: a forensic scientist, for instance, demonstrates how crime evidence is researched to determine the identity of a victim or perpetrator. Further investigation into semiotics, sociology and psychoanalysis paves the way to a scientifically formed theory about identity and identification.

Identities

'The design bears the signature of the designer. The designer is an author. On the other hand, he derives his (self-)image from the efficacy with which he interprets the desired self-image of his client for a more or less given public. The designer interprets and reinforces someone else's story. The modern designer therefore determines himself, but is determined by others as well.'
Hugues Boekraad, Annual Report, Post-St.Joost 1999, p. 137

'The forensic portrait is an important means of making the leap from deconstruction to construction, and then to communication. Moreover, through the detective work that the other students have to do, the exercise has the character of a challenging game. It stimulates discussion among the students.'
Interview with Edith Gruson, 11 November, 1999

'Of course we are also ultimately interested in the personality of the designer, in the colour he brings to his work. The adage that Cassandre used to describe the designer as a 'telegraph operator' is false, but to arrive at what that personality is, you must first identify the problem of the accepted identity.'
Interview with Hugues Boekraad, 11 November, 1999

IDENTITIES
Theme I
Forensic Self Portrait
SUZANNE VAN GRIENSVEN
& Imaginary Portrait
Three Squares

ITEMS

1. Choco Pops wrappers
My favourite breakfast

2. Delial Cream
I use Delial every day.
I also like the bottle (the colours
and the letters).

3. Wookie
I collect things from Star Wars
and this one is a really sweet
representation for the tough
Chewbacca

4. Shirt
I made it myself, years ago.
I like (animal) logos that are very
simple but good.

5. Frame with two photographs
My boyfriend and me as children,
each in a school photograph, coincidentally with the same background

6. Sandwich packaging
Made by my boyfriend...
especially for me

7. Badges from skateboard clothing
I like this world.

8. Piece of a skateboard
From a special skateboard broken
at a project I made up

9. Cards (from my collection)
Nice for dreaming away

IDENTITIES
Theme I
Forensic Self Portrait
HEIKE CZERNER
& Imaginary Portrait
Three Squares

ITEMS

THE PRESENT
1. Box with 6 drawers
2. 4 Passport photographs

THE PAST
3. 1 slide transparency
4. 1 ticket
5. 1 ship-in-a-bottle
6. 1 button
7. 7 slips (of paper)

1. Box with 6 drawers
– Depending on my mood, I tend
  to put my whole 'life' in boxes
  and take it out of the boxes
  again, rearranging it – into new
  'boxes' – according to different
  situations, habits, attitudes.
– It is my nature to collect things,
  to sort things, to give them some
  kind of order.
– the metaphor depends on what
  the boxes mean (to me):
    • give order
    • to put some things in or take
      them out, change, turn, switch
      them in any case with objects,
      thoughts, problems, aims, me
      as a person

2. 4 Passport photographs
– from my first student exchange
  in Italy shows my feelings on
  finding myself in a new situation
– stands for me as something that
  has changed, something without
  any order or security, something
  flexible altered into something
  that has to be given a new
  structure
– a look at my authentic character,
  with the several faces that I have

3. 1 slide transparency
– something that fascinates me in
  form and content, a border
  where something new begins
– shows my work in photographic
  and typographic form
– an element from a school exam
– my way of thinking in abstractions

4. 1 ticket
– stands for my lovable island,
  where I spend all of my holidays
– the island as a metaphor for my
  harmony, my point of view

5. 1 ship-in-a-bottle
– comes from a friend accepting
  my character, my work about
  natural and philosophical islands
– depends on, or stands for the
  people I need in my life, as a
  personal island

6. 1 button
– moods, making plans, being
  perfect, being 'straight-on',
  negative aspects
– also as a reflection of myself

7. 7 slips (of paper)
– my future, my situation now
– making plans, organizing everything, making lists of it all
  giving a structure to everything,
  putting my old life into the 'new'.
  New developments change my
  habits. Something that appeared
  foreign leads to a new perspective.

*but everything again goes into
boxes…*

IDENTITIES
Theme I
Forensic Self Portrait
HEIKO LIEBEL
& Imaginary Portrait
Three Squares

ITEMS

1. **14 cigarette paper packs (empty)**
2. **1 pack of cigarette papers (half empty)**
3. **1 wallet**
   including:
   - 4 used train tickets
   - 1 lottery ticket
   - 1 registration statement from the SWB
   - 1 student card from FH Wurzburg (valid through 30 September)
   - 2 pieces of paper with phone numbers on them
   - 1 dentist bonuschart
   - some money
   - 2 'Euro-Passes', (1 German & 1 Dutch)
   - 2 credit cards (1 expired, 1 valid)
   - 2 library cards
   - 2 German train tickets (1 expired, 1valid)
   - 2 video shop customer cards
   - 1 health insurance card
   - 1 ISIC card (expired)
   - 3 telephone cards (2 Dutch, 1 German)
   - 1 photograph
   - 1 youth hostel card
   - 1 ID card
   - 1 driver's licence
   - 1 key
   - 1 piece of paper with an e-mail address

My last two months were dominated by moving. Moving out of my flat in Wurzburg and moving to Breda – which included working during the week for an advertising agency to get enough money for a few months, and living with my parents because it was close to the place where I worked. In the weekends I went back to Wurzburg to meet friends and have lots of farewell drinks and farewell barbecues with them, and of course to pack my things in cardboard boxes and write on the outside what was on the inside.

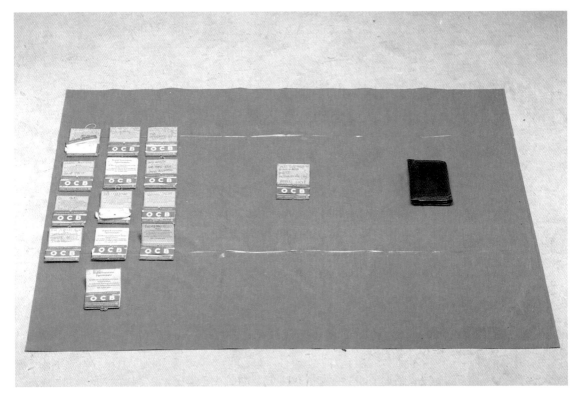

I threw out most of the things I didn't need, but not everything. When I arrived in Breda I realized there were three places I hadn't cleaned out: my car, my backpack and my wallet. So when I dug through the piles of stuff, I found some surprises. Most of the things I found are relics of my life in Germany, but some point to my 'new' life in Holland.

1. 14 cigarette paper packs (empty)

I used to write down phone numbers and addresses on these cigarette paper packs. It was handy. They have this rubber band and you could hang them on the wall over your phone. Once they changed the design of the packaging. The rubber band was on the other side and you had to hang them upside down. After a few months they changed it back. Maybe people were complaining about this upside- down thing. When I was moving out of my old flat I just packed all those packages in my backpack. I wanted to write down all the numbers in them into my Filofax. However, I forgot about doing that. I just carried the stuff around with me for a month. Some numbers have changed, and there are also numbers I never call. I don't know if I should get rid of those packages. They look quite nice pinned to the wall.

2. 1 pack of cigarette papers (half empty)

When we were drunk we had this idea of building up our own studio. We had the name written on this pack:

[fɔ: 'dʌblu: ænd ai]

We were fascinated by the different possibilities of writing that. We had big plans but they never came to be. So we just agreed on signing everything one of us creates with 'a division of www & I ', give it that conspiratorial flavour.

3. 1 wallet

There really is too much useless stuff in my wallet. Why not dump those train tickets (2x Dusseldorf-Wurzburg, 2x Wurzburg-Dusseldorf)? I only went through Dusseldorf to travel on to Breda to look for an apartment. Once on the way back I missed my connection, so I had to wait in Frankfurt for two hours for the last train to Wurzburg. I met this Russian guy, however, who was studying in Leiden.

The lottery ticket
During the last six weeks, I have played the 'Lotto' together with a friend of mine. I was always hoping to get the jackpot so I could quit my shit job at this advertising agency. Well we did win, even twice: 70 Marks in all.

SWB Registration Statement
I could have found a better way to use that 50 guilders…

Student card from Wurzburg
Officially I am still there…

2 pieces of paper with phone numbers
The one, Anja Mayer, is a friend of a friend, studying in Maastricht for half a year. I even called here once. The other is the dial-through to my boss at Publicis, the agency I worked for. It was like prostitution…
I was young and needed the dough. There is another number on the pack. I don't know whose it is.

Bonuschart
In Germany, you have to have this. You have to go to the dentist at least once a year. I went… and that really was the last thing I did in my home town before I left for Holland.

Money
It is a kind of necessity, which you can also say is true for the international train passes, the credit cards (although I should chuck the

expired one, and also the expired Bahn Card) and the telephone cards (though I don't really know if there is still anything on them).

The ID Card, the Driver's Licence, the Youth Hostel Card
Could be useful…

Maybe I should get rid of the *Wurzburg library card* and also the *video store customer card*.

The funny thing is that the only thing in my wallet which indicates that I live in Breda is this card from the *'Last Page Cultvideotheque'*.

Oh yes, this expired *ISIC card* reminds me of my student exchange term in England.

I am still carrying a *photograph of my ex-girlfriend* with me. We split up in May and I never bothered to take the photograph out of my wallet. It doesn't really disturb me. I only feel a bit strange when my new girlfriend gets a glimpse of the photograph.

The key
I have had this key since I was a little boy. I always had this secret drawer where I could hide stuff from my parents. First I kept chocolate and comic books in there. When I got older it was a nice hiding place for cigarettes, small bottles of alcohol and the occasional porno magazine. Now it is pretty much out of use. I still keep it locked and carry the key around with me… maybe just for old times' sake.

The e-mail address
The irony of fate: this is the e-mail address of my girlfriend's ex-boy-friend.

IDENTITIES
Theme I
Forensic Self Portrait
**& Imaginary Portrait
(Fictional Character)
MINKE THEMANS**
Three Squares

'The Death of a Man'

A Character Description and the Life of my Imaginary Portrait

1. X is a vain man of middle age. He is a family doctor with his own practice. He feels that practising medicine is mostly about writing out prescriptions, which is usually enough to satisfy his patients. He is more interested in man's spiritual aspects and his reading therefore includes many books on such subjects as Rogerian Therapy. X's interest in Rogerian Therapy and sexology has not only evolved from his interest in his patients, but also from questions about his own sexuality.

2. X finds delight in occasionally dressing up as a woman. He prefers to do this in hotels, places where no one knows him. At first, it was limited to a single evening a month, but the urge increased. He wanted to appear to the rest of the world as a woman.

3. More and more frequently, he dresses in women's clothes, spending hours making himself up and preening. He makes his decision. He wants a sex change operation. X writes himself prescriptions for the hormones he needs to achieve his ideal and registers at the regional public health institute for psychiatric support.

4. All this can no longer be combined with his general practice as a physician. X decides to stop practising medicine. He plans a trip to New York to pass the time until his operation. Here, in anonymity, he builds himself a new life as a woman.

5. Finally, X returns to Holland to undergo his operation.

IDENTITIES
Theme I
Forensic Self Portrait
& Imaginary Portrait
(Fictional Character)
MATTHEW SANABRIA
Three Squares

ITEMS
1. ring with keys
2. razor
3. shaving cream
4. wallet
5. assorted cans
6. eye-glasses
7. glasses case
8. fork
9. spoon
10. teapot
11. teabag
12. matches
13. salt & pepper shaker
14. glass
15. wp
16. alarm clock

Alzheimer's disease

A condition that occurs late in life and worsens with time, in which the brain cells degenerate. It is accompanied by memory loss, physical decline and confusion.
– AMA. Health Insight –

Alzheimer's Disease

A progressive, neuro-degenerative disease characterized by loss of function and death of nerve cells in several areas of the brain, leading to loss of cognitive function such as memory and language. The cause of nerve cell death is unknown, but the cells are recognized by the appearance of an unusual helical protein filament in the nerve cells (neurofibrillary tangles) and by degeneration in cortical regions of brain, especially frontal and temporal lobes. Alzheimer's disease is the most common cause of dementia.
– On-Line Medical Dictionary –

Let me begin by telling you my name. I'm John and my life has come to the point where I have to write down some things before I forget them. Before I forget how to read.

I woke up this morning at six, feeling a bit uneasy, it was still dark

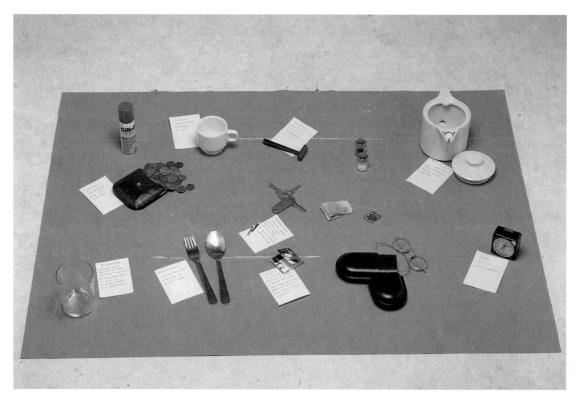

outside. I turned my head towards the window and still could name the things I saw: the barometer, the alarm clock on the sill by the glass of water with my denture in it. The best thing was that I still knew what they were for. I put my robe on and went downstairs to have breakfast. Before going down, I stopped for some time to look at the pictures on the small table by the stairs. I could recognize everybody and remembered all the situations almost as if they had happened yesterday. The pictures are of my childhood, back in the thirties. I then looked up and saw my image in the mirror. I almost didn't know who it was. How my hair has thinned, not to mention how white it is.

Down in the kitchen I thought that if I could just remember what all those things were called and what they were for, I could prove to my family that I can still take care of myself. So I started opening drawers and cabinets and naming every-thing. I saw the toaster and knew what to do with it. I even got the coffee going in the Melita machine. I remembered those sharp objects were called knives and they are used to chop and cut. I saw a pan and knew it was for frying, so I got some bacon going while I beat the eggs and sliced a tomato. I then put some slices of bread in the toaster and was quite glad to know how to use it (it is simple, by the way). I sat down, very proud of having made breakfast by myself, and of even having been able to use the can opener so I could make some juice. Afterwards I got all the dishes into the washer (though it took some time to get it started) and went into the living room to finish my cup of coffee and read the newspaper. I felt in a very good mood, so I decided to leave the paper unread and call my son to tell him the good news: breakfast

by myself. But then I thought that, while it still was fresh in my mind, I should write it down and make a plan of the kitchen, to always carry with me, just in case. Then I would call my son.

With this portrait, rather than representing what John did after-wards, my intention is to show what having Alzheimer's could be like. There is a loss of immediate memory, so people with Alzheimer's find themselves having breakfast twice a day, for they can't remember that they have already eaten. Or finding the water in the tub too hot and, while forgetting, stepping in any-way. Oddly enough, past memory is enhanced and they remember things that had been long forgotten, things which become a part of their conversations with people who were probably not even in the original situation.

IDENTITIES
Theme I
Forensic Self Portrait
& Imaginary Portrait
(Fictional Character)
SHERI PRESLER
Three Squares

ITEMS

1. **Burger King bag**
   container for an ill-fated meal
2. **French fry container**
   all contents are gone, including
   the patient's finger – fingers
   and fries are a similar shape
3. **Hamburger wrapper**
   part of the ill-fated meal
4. **ketchup label**
   mistake this for blood
5. **gloves (minus 1 finger)**
   premeditated self-amputation
   of finger
6. **finger in a jar**
   autopsy results
7. **Knakwurst sausages**
   food resembling a finger

THERAPY LOG BOOK
Session #1 My therapist suggested
that I keep a journal to reflect on
our conversations after each visit.
I am still so disturbed by what is
happening to me that I can't quite
put it into words. Perhaps I'll soon

come to terms with my accidents.
Until then, I have to learn to deal
with this situation. You know how
when your baby is born, you count
to make sure it has ten fingers and
ten toes? I mean five on each hand,
so twenty all together? If they're
all there, the parents can enjoy a
sigh of relief. If not, well, I'm sure
it's not a pleasant experience.

Session #2 Sure, I've had my
occasional accidents. Being a
graphic designer, I've had nume-
rous encounters with the Xacto
knife. I've seen the tendons in my
index finger, and I've cut half-way
through my middle finger with
a bread knife. Initially, I would
very calmly think, 'Oh God, I know
I cut myself,' because the slice was
so sharp that I didn't really feel
any pain. Then I'd look at the
damage and try to figure out a
way to avoid having to go to the
emergency room to get stitches.
I never needed them.

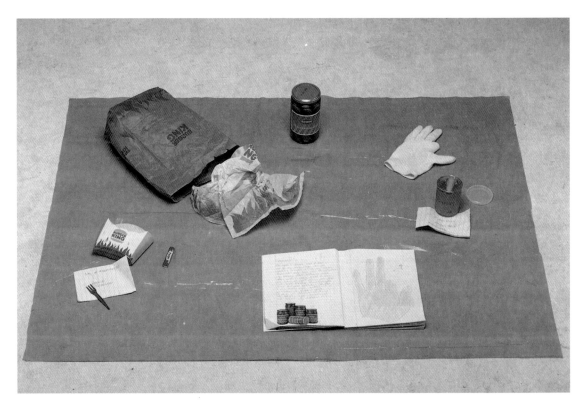

These incidents stick out most in my mind. I managed to avoid the Lidocaine and needles and go about my business, taking care not to look at my wounds. I can watch surgery being performed on someone else with no problem, but when I see my own 'insides', I tend to feel sick to my stomach. I've always had an aversion to larger knives, but the Xacto has made me increasingly squeamish lately.

Session #3 This week I dreamt that I had cut off my whole finger –or at least I thought it was my finger. There have only been two times when my dreams have actually come true, and I mean those dreams you have at night when you sleep, not 'wish' dreams like when you blow out your birthday candles. I am hoping that this is not a premonition of some sort. I saw 'The Blair Witch Project' not too long ago – maybe that is the reason why I dreamt this…

Session #4 It happened again this week. But this time, I dreamt that I had a confrontation in the kitchen with a very large knife while I was making lunch. But instead of being shocked, instead of screaming, I put my finger on a bun, squirted some ketchup on it and served it to my friend for lunch. Just as he was about to take a bite, I woke up very confused. I counted my fingers and I still had ten.

Session #5 I can't take this anymore. These dreams are disturbingly strange. This time I put my finger on a bun, just like a hot dog and took one bite, then another – and another, until there was nothing left but a stump. There was no blood. I proceeded to lick the salty taste from my fingers, but when I got to my index finger on my left hand, there was nothing there and I was bleeding uncontrollably. I woke up, petrified – I can't stand to be alone anymore. I can't stand knives and I am afraid of anything resembling a finger. I know it's not real, but sometimes I can't help but think it's real. It feels real. . .

PHYSICIAN'S NOTES
regarding case #0624154930

Patient #0624154930 is a chronic sleepwalker, observed in my clinic for seven consecutive nights from 1 September, 1999. Suffers from night sweats. Each night the sleepwalking session included a trip to the refrigerator, along with the preparation of a meal. The patient appeared completely coherent. However, if interrupted in any way by a strange sound, for example, or if something was lying on the floor in the patient's path, a series of odd, sometimes dangerous reactions would follow. The patient would become self-threatening, but was not a threat to others.
This morning, 28 September, 1999, the subject was found lying facedown on his kitchen table with a Burger King sack, a hamburger wrapper and an empty french-fry container. The index finger on his left hand was bitten off at the metatarsal joint. It appears that the patient was involved in a sleepwalking episode at the time and chewed off his own finger, perhaps mistaking it for a french-fry. This would be consistent with the dream episodes experienced by the patient as they were described to me in therapy, as well as recorded in his journal. Also found on the kitchen table next to the subject was a jar of knackwurst sausages and a pair of gloves with the index finger of the left glove specially tailored to accommodate an amputated index finger. It is difficult to say exactly when this tailoring session occurred, but it seems apparent that the patient subconsciously pre-meditated his actions of last night.

Signed,

The Doctor

AUTOPSY RESULTS
regarding case #0624154930

We recovered the finger (specimen #0624154930). Surprisingly, it had not been digested – it was still in its original state and was bitten off only at the metatarsal joint. All other tests revealed nothing unusual.

Signed,

The Forensic Doc

IDENTITIES
Theme I
Forensic Self Portrait
& Imaginary Portrait
Three Squares

Synonymous Tools The exercise is so deceptively simple that it seems incomprehensible that the three squares are in fact an impossible task. The three basic tools of the graphic designer – a typeset text, an image and a colour, normally fused together in the design work – are now presented as separate elements of a coherent message. For this is the question: can you select or make a text, an image and a colour, each of which imparts the same message, or in other words, is a synonym of the others? Is a single means or medium, for example, a colour, sufficient to get a message across, a message that subsequently has its equivalent in an image and then also in a text? The size of the panel – one square metre – determines the tone of the message. It is too large for the private sketchbook and too small for a public billboard. Here too, the idea is deconstruction, and again, the 'others' are the ones who must interpret the tale. The maker puts it in code and the remaining students then decode a message that has been prevented from bearing the personal accent of the designer's handwriting. Both learn to regard looking as a linguistic activity. What they see has to be expressed in the form of argument.

The exercise is repeated in three stages. The first is with found text, image and colour. The second time around, text and image have to be of the student's own making, and in the final stage, they must be produced by hand. Each time, the theme is that borderline between private and public, a division that in the practice of mass communications, is difficult to draw. The public domain increasingly penetrates into the private, and even the distinction between the sender and the receiver can almost no longer be drawn. In the Post-St. Joost curriculum, however, the bridge has now been built to the second major theme of the programme: the urban, public setting.

Encoding/Decoding

'In the deciphering process, remarkable cultural differences appear. A Polish student will read a forensic portrait or the three squares entirely differently than an Irish student, and the Irishman again reads it differently than a Dutch student.'
*Interview with Edith Gruson,
11 November, 1999*

Theory

'Understanding theory and the development of a useable language offer a model to counter the tongue-tied speechlessness and the scrapping that currently domi- nate discussion about design and communication.'
*Interview with Gerard Hadders,
18 November, 1999*

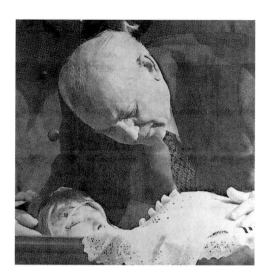

IDENTITIES
Theme I
Forensic Self Portrait
& Imaginary Portrait
**Three Squares
(Found Image, Text
and Colour)
JEROEN KLOMP**

last goodbye

Colour: purple

IDENTITIES

Forensic Self Portrait
& Imaginary Portrait

**Three Squares
(Created Image and Text)
PETER ZUIDERWIJK**

Schaamstreek

Colour: skin

IDENTITIES
Theme I
Forensic Self Portrait
& Imaginary Portrait
**Three Squares
(Created Image and Text)
RUTH LEEDE**

Ik zoek altijd naar een plek

Met veel ruimte   Zodat ik mijn   Eigen spullen om   Me heen

heb en ik
lekker onderuit
K AN ZITTE   N
PAS WANNEER

Het
Echt druk   Is haal ik   Mijn   Spullen

WEG EN MAAK   IK
Plaats

Colour: red

IDENTITIES
Theme I
Forensic Self Portrait
& Imaginary Portrait
**Three Squares
(Hand-made Image,
Text and Colour)
KATHERINE SZETO**

*I never did like
that Camilla.
Diana's always
been my favourite.*

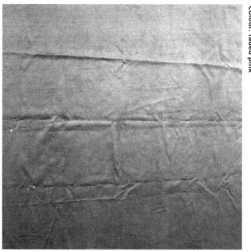

Colour: faded pink

IDENTITIES
Theme I
Forensic Self Portrait
& Imaginary Portrait
**Three Squares
(Hand-made Image,
Text and Colour)**
PETER ZUIDERWIJK

Colour: copper

PUBLIC SPHERE AND URBAN SPACE
Theme II
Visual Essay

To an important degree, the complexity of today's visual culture determines the graphic designer's workplace. His capacity to analyze and register that complexity is a 'conditio sine qua non' for valuable intervention by designers. To reach that goal, complicated structures must first be unravelled into clear denominators in order to again seek out the complexity. The city – along the lines of Paris, New Delhi, Rotterdam or a small town like Nagele in Holland's Northeast Polder – provides a useful metaphor for the essences of communication. It does so in a context of values temporary and permanent, of long-term planning and incidents, of comfort and lack of safety, of wear-and-tear and renewal, of ideologies and pragmatism, of the private and the public. In this context, Rem Koolhaas's designs for 'EuraLille' are juxtaposed with the extravaganza of the EuroDisney city in the Paris suburbs. A city, which establishes set patterns of encounters, is in fact the design of a communicative environment. In this light, it is a Fundgrube, a veritable treasure chest for graphic designers.

Just as public domain and accessibility play an important role in the blossoming or the dissolution of a city, so it also does for the accessibility of virtual domains. The moment there is no longer a relationship between the experience of physical space and the mental understanding of cyberspace, the inhabitant of the digital city finds himself lost, wandering about in a ghost town. On the basis of research on urban spaces – both the morphological structure of the city and the social space within the urban environment – the designer's field of vision expands into his own everyday living environment. A framework arises in which to study such elements as time (or change) and space in the design process.

Architecture and urban planning also offer another dimension. In these disciplines, the use of language and theory has been more highly developed than is to date the case in industrial or graphic design. At Post-St. Joost, this theoretical context comes along on the excursions undertaken in this thematic framework. Architecture in its written form is as much a part of the man-made environment as the concrete, steel and glass in which it has materialized. Those who have learned to recognize its value will no longer be content with the sell-out of the work of graphic designers as the most individualistic expression of the individualist artist, the mystical, uncontrollable, big-blue-eyed genius who charms his clients into everlasting belief. In architecture, and indeed, in product development, such an attitude is no longer tenable. In these fields, the process must be transparent and accessible in order for decisions about changes to be made. The form of the professionalism involved here is the cornerstone of the third and final theme of proposal and counterproposal.

**PUBLIC SPHERE
AND URBAN SPACE**
Theme II
**Visual Essay on Complexity
in Reading Design
GERARD HADDERS**

This is not the history of AEG's design

(Just some of the results)

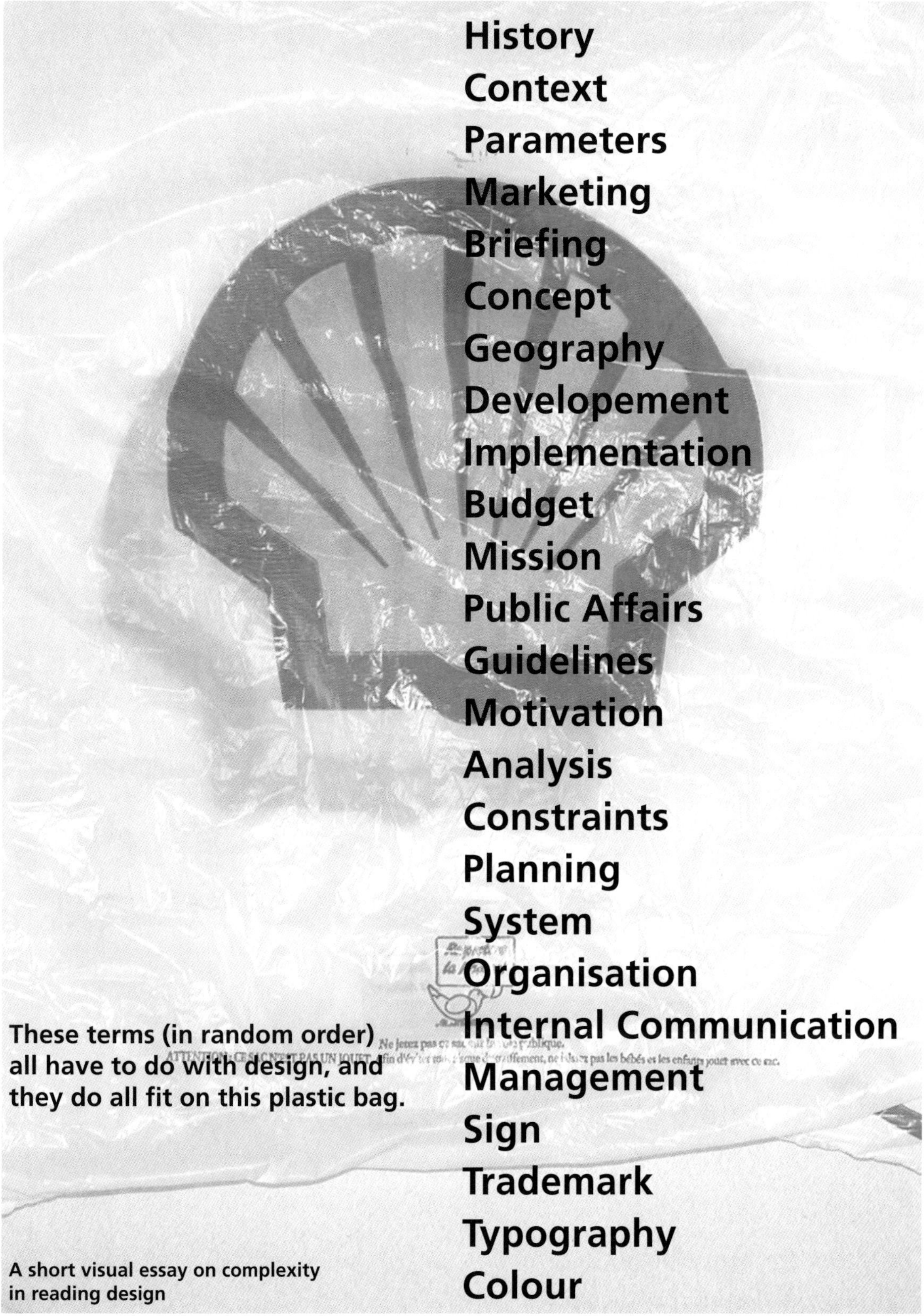

History
Context
Parameters
Marketing
Briefing
Concept
Geography
Developement
Implementation
Budget
Mission
Public Affairs
Guidelines
Motivation
Analysis
Constraints
Planning
System
Organisation
Internal Communication
Management
Sign
Trademark
Typography
Colour

These terms (in random order) all have to do with design, and they do all fit on this plastic bag.

A short visual essay on complexity in reading design

Design and complexity
Model

Thinking, form and space made visible

O.M.A., Model for the Bibliothèque de France competition

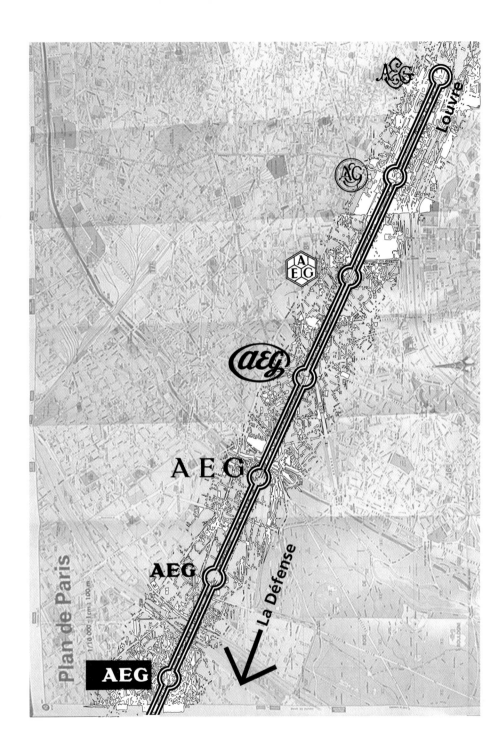

Design and complexity
History

Urban development equation

The 'Paris Axis walk'

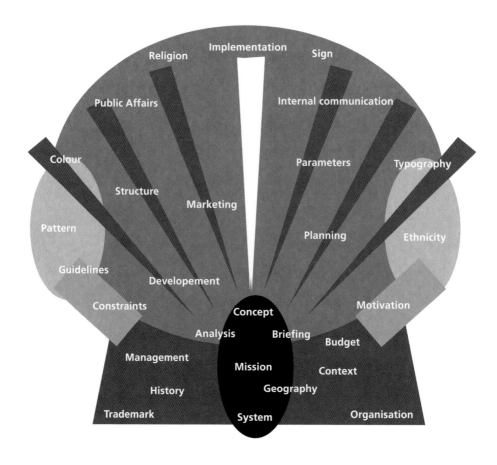

Design and complexity
Model model

From the series 'Absolute TM™'

Implementation

Colour

Constraints

History

Ethnicity

Planning

Geography

System

Marketing

Organisation

Management

Parameters

Analysis

Budget

Sign

Briefing

Trademark

Pattern

Mission

Context

Motivation

Concept

Typography

Structure

Developement

Public Affairs

Guidelines

Religion

Internal communication

Design and complexity
Epidemic model

From the series 'Absolute TM™'

Design and complexity
'Bricolage' model

From the series 'Absolute TM™'

Design and complexity
Labyrinthine model

From the series 'Absolute TM™'

Design and complexity

History

Urban development equation

From the series 'Absolute TM™'

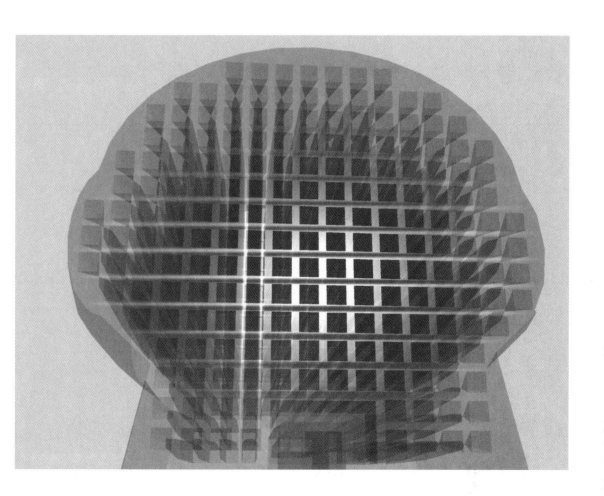

Design and complexity

Architecture as model

Architecture can be perceived in its history and complexity

From the series 'Absolute TM™'

PROPOSAL AND COUNTER-PROPOSAL
Theme III
Visual Essay
Poetry in Urban Spaces

Designing in the professional context is a form of moral and strategic action, of moves and countermoves, of establishing boundaries and going beyond boundaries. In their deliberations, designers not only have to be capable of claiming their own ground (the role developed under the identities theme) and able to intervene on a believable, convincing foundation of registration and analysis (the urban space theme), but they must also operate on equal footing with their client. The client's proposal must be answered with a response, a counterproposal that is backed up by sound argument.

The designer must be able to take responsibility for that counterproposal, his thoughts and actions perceptible and transparent. This means that the student must be able to function outside the protected environment of the academy or his fellow designers. He requires mastery of the methods that apply within all the various positions that he may be expected to assume in the 'real' world, and must learn to be in command of the systems underlying those roles. Here, a style will no longer come to his aid. That style, at best, can be of help within the highly affective niches in which Dutch graphic design has preferred to move: the museums, the art circuits and perhaps the design of CD covers.

Visual Essay In order to force the breakthrough into other, more complex domains – a necessary remedy against design getting worn out – the medium of the visual essay has been given a new lease on life. This form of scenario development has already been in use in American visual communications for some 50 years, in order to design communications models. It offers the presentation of a problem, the possible solutions and the whole trajectory linking the two.

For educational purposes, the visual essay proves an ideal connection between theory and practice, because it is not medium-specific or geared to results, but focussed on process. The underlying problem is presented in as broad a manner as possible and is just as broadly investigated, even when the initial assignment was not so inclined. In fact, the essay begins with a database, a shoebox full of options and research material. The visual essay then documents the development of thought, records interim solutions, research results and images, argues the ideas and illustrates the context of the problem. It is not the inner expression that forms the core of the essay, which

Visual Essay

'We want the designers out of the tail end of the communications process. But they then need the tools to learn to think strategically. That is the only way we will be able to exercise more influence or power.'
Interview with Gerard Hadders, 18 November, 1999

'Practising their profession has often become too uninteresting for well-trained designers.'
Interview with Hugues Boekraad, 28 October, 1999

remains 'under construction', without leading to a single end result, but its potential for being put to the test by the outside world. Being able to think in terms of multiple images prevents the client from having a solidified, definitive solution plunked down on his desk. For students and professional designers, the visual essay moreover gives insight into one's own motives and actions. The end result is the public statement of proof of a designing process and at the same time serves as a proposal for deliberation, or as the report of an investigation and a platform for communications on a number of relevant subjects.

PROPOSAL AND
COUNTER-PROPOSAL
Theme III
Visual Essay
FLOOR HOUBEN
Poetry in Urban Spaces

poëzie in de
stedelijke ruimte
van Breda

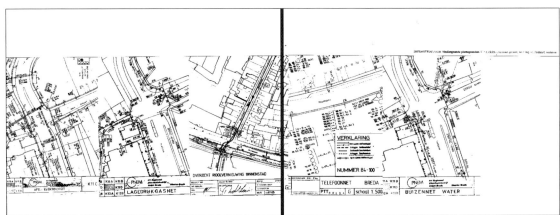

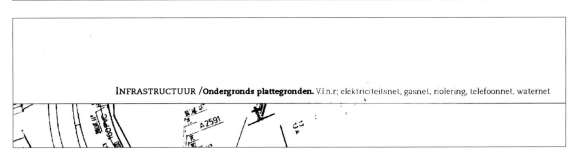

INFRASTRUCTUUR /Ondergronds plattegronden. V.l.n.r; elektriciteitsnet, gasnet, riolering, telefoonnet, waternet

Visualisatie van themabuurten

Aangesloten op spraak in van thematische kruinmerking in de nieuwe wijken aan een zich kunnen voorstellen dat door themas op een bijzondere wijze onder de aandacht van de bewoners kan worden gebracht. Naast planten, daarin en bloemen worden aan groepen woken aan een bewoon daar ze te verbruinen op visualisatiemodus. Een manier om een grote beleidig tussen straten in bakenseraken in het ibeeit weergeven van elementen die met de themas verheeren om. Op de linkingspagina die het hysteriepics en de Sirmeelseeremaat woonten van voorverleerlingen. Op de aethidologies zijn werken van Pieter Bringhof en Jeroen Bosch aangebaardt in de derletterStedt straten.

Kleursysteem

Een variant van de thematische naamgeving zou een systeem kunnen zijn waarin men uitsluitend kleuren gebruikt. Wijken zouden zich dan onderscheiden door verschillen in kleur. Een aanvaarmelding zou dan als volgt kunnen zijn. Cyaan 1315 of Karmijnrood 3145. Een leuke bijkomstigheid is dat men in dit systeem naast de talige aanduiding, de kleuren in het visuaberld kan aanbrengen. De straatranden zouden kunnen worden voorzien van de desbetreffende kleur waardoor een groter herkenbaarheid ontstaat.

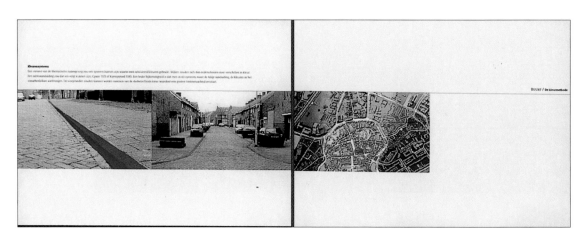

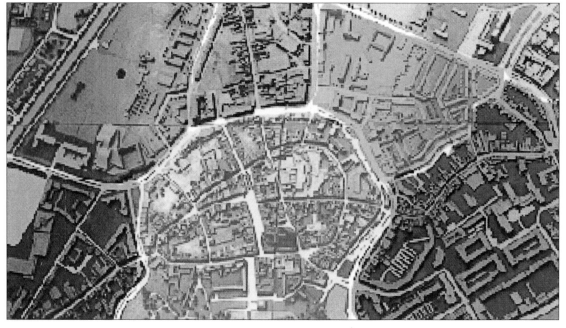

STRAATNAAMBORD / Voorend no.3

Het vervangen van straatnamen

In mijn alle-zintuin-oriënterende-wandeling door de wijk Zandberg leerde ik verschillende geschikte locaties tegen waar het plaatsen van, mijn idee-lijke plan is een zowel mogelijk vast te houden aan de communicatie-omschrijvingsproces van deze referentiekeuzer keuzer maar wel te spitzer met met met convementente plaatsing steun.

VOORSTEL / Onderzoek naar geschikte locaties. Via v. Parkstraat, Wilhelminasingel, Sorenolaan, Zandberg/Maaweistraat

VOORSTEL / Onderzoek naar geschikte locaties. V.l.n.r. 2 maal Wilhelminapark, Koestraat, Johan Willem Frisolaan

VOORSTEL / Johan Willem Friesolaan

Veel verschillende
moeilijke namen heeft het
gras van de lente.

Bonk

PROPOSAL AND COUNTER-PROPOSAL
Theme III
Visual Essay
ALAN FITZPATRICK
Poetry in Urban Spaces

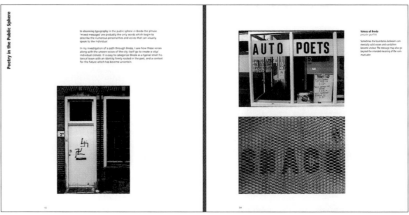

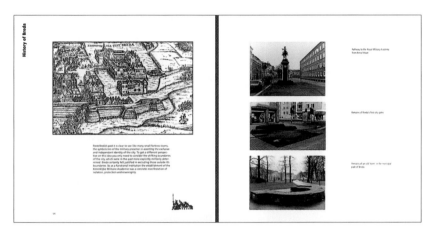

From Breda's past it is clear to see like many small fortress towns, the symbolism of the military presence in asserting the exclusive and independent identity of the city. To get a different perspective on this idea you only need to consider the shifting boundaries of the city, which were in the past more explicitly military determined. Breda certainly felt justified in excluding those outside it's boundaries. So as a functional institution the establishment of the Koninklijke Militaire Academie was a concrete manifestation of isolation, protection and sovereignty.

Pathway to the Royal Military Academy from Anna Straat

Remains of Breda's first city gates

Remains of an old 'town' in the municipal park of Breda

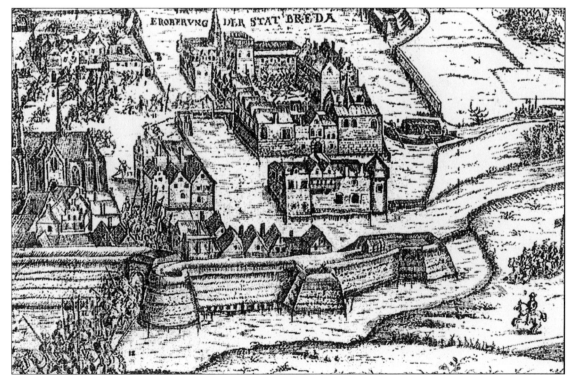

Here the two main connecting passageways into and out of the 'military zone'.
The first comes from the municipal park
and the other links the academy with the
city centre.

As a foreigner, The Royal Military Academy struck me as a curious expression of the accumulation
of Breda's military and political history and it's present significance and context in a changing small
historical town. I also wanted to question the apparently necessary distance between military personnel and the public.

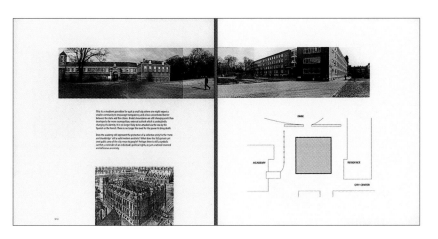

This is a modern paradise for such a small city where one might expect a smaller community to encourage transparency and a less concentrated barrier between the state and the citizen. Breda's boundaries are still changing and it has developed a far more cosmopolitan, external outlook which is undoubtedly changing it's identity. It is no longer likely to be attacked via the sea by the Spanish or the French. There is no longer the need for the power to bring death.

Does the academy still represent the protection of a collective unity? Is the 'mote and drawbridge' still a valid modern aesthetic? What does this fully private yet semi-public area of the city mean to people? Perhaps there is still a symbolic comfort, a reminder of an individual's political rights, or, just a rational reserved and defensive anonimity.

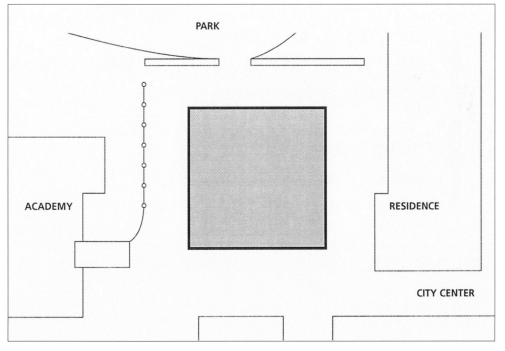

PARK

ACADEMY

RESIDENCE

CITY CENTER

what a joy to know,
even when we can't see or hear you,
that you are around,

though very few of you
find us worth looking at,
unless we come too close.

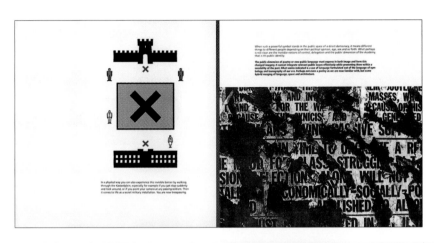

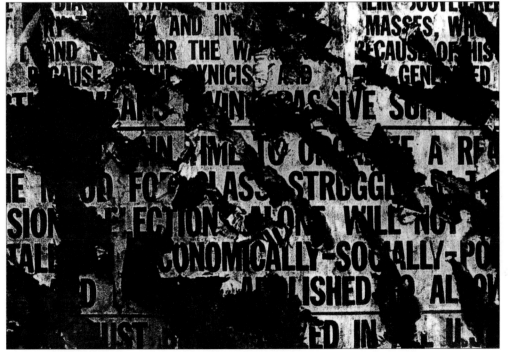

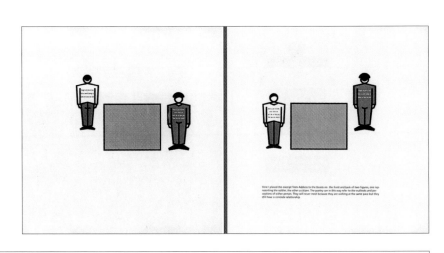

Here I placed the excerpt from *Address to the Beasts* on the front and back of two figures, one representing the soldier, the other a citizen. The poetry can in this way refer to the outlooks and perceptions of either person. They will never meet because they are walking at the same pace but they still have a concrete relationship

though very few of you
find us worth looking at,
unless we come too close

what a joy to know,
even when we
can't see or hear you,
that you are around

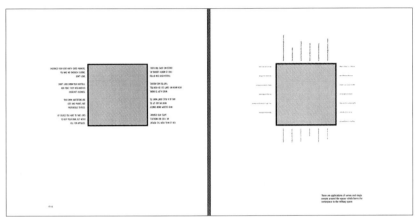

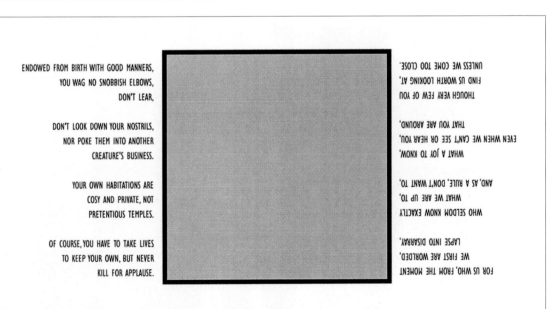

ENDOWED FROM BIRTH WITH GOOD MANNERS,
YOU WAG NO SNOBBISH ELBOWS,
DON'T LEAR,

DON'T LOOK DOWN YOUR NOSTRILS,
NOR POKE THEM INTO ANOTHER
CREATURE'S BUSINESS.

YOUR OWN HABITATIONS ARE
COSY AND PRIVATE, NOT
PRETENTIOUS TEMPLES.

OF COURSE, YOU HAVE TO TAKE LIVES
TO KEEP YOUR OWN, BUT NEVER
KILL FOR APPLAUSE.

UNLESS WE COME TOO CLOSE.
FIND US WORTH LOOKING AT,
THOUGH VERY FEW OF YOU

THAT YOU ARE AROUND,
EVEN WHEN WE CAN'T SEE OR HEAR YOU,
WHAT A JOY TO KNOW,

AND, AS A RULE, DON'T WANT TO,
WHAT WE ARE UP TO,
WHO SELDOM KNOW EXACTLY

LAPSE INTO DISARRAY,
WE FIRST ARE WORLDED,
FOR US WHO, FROM THE MOMENT

PROPOSAL AND COUNTER-PROPOSAL
Theme III
Visual Essay
STEFFEN MAAS
Poetry in Urban Spaces

Tree
Boom

right: *Frantisek Kupka:*
Filosofische Architectuur/
Philosophical Architecture (1913)

tolerance
tolerantie

below: *Miniature train in the Prater, Vienna*

traces
sporen

below: *The map of the park can also be read as an Indian story told in pictures*

space
ruimte

below: *Michaelangelo's design for the Capitol Plaza in Rome (1569)*

Onder: *Liliputbaan in het Prater, Wenen*

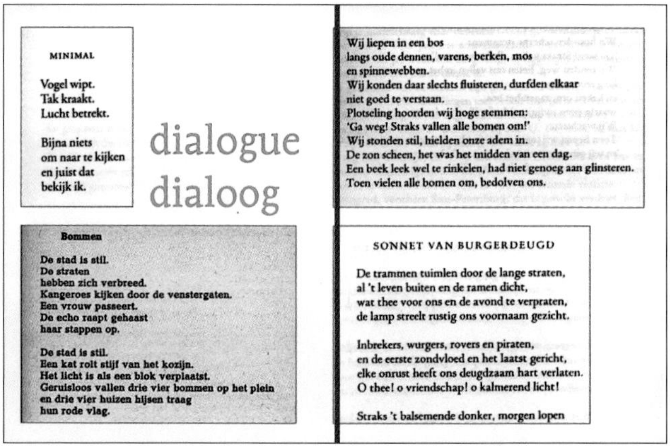

MINIMAL

Vogel wipt.
Tak kraakt.
Lucht betrekt.

Bijna niets
om naar te kijken
en juist dat
bekijk ik.

dialogue
dialoog

Bommen

De stad is stil.
De straten
hebben zich verbreed.
Kangeroes kijken door de venstergaten.
Een vrouw passeert.
De echo raapt gehaast
haar stappen op.

De stad is stil.
Een kat rolt stijf van het kozijn.
Het licht is als een blok verplaatst.
Geruisloos vallen drie vier bommen op het plein
en drie vier huizen hijsen traag
hun rode vlag.

Wij liepen in een bos
langs oude dennen, varens, berken, mos
en spinnewebben.
Wij konden daar slechts fluisteren, durfden elkaar
niet goed te verstaan.
Plotseling hoorden wij hoge stemmen:
'Ga weg! Straks vallen alle bomen om!'
Wij stonden stil, hielden onze adem in.
De zon scheen, het was het midden van een dag.
Een beek leek wel te rinkelen, had niet genoeg aan glinsteren.
Toen vielen alle bomen om, bedolven ons.

SONNET VAN BURGERDEUGD

De trammen tuimlen door de lange straten,
al 't leven buiten en de ramen dicht,
wat thee voor ons en de avond te verpraten,
de lamp streelt rustig ons voornaam gezicht.

Inbrekers, wurgers, rovers en piraten,
en de eerste zondvloed en het laatst gericht,
elke onrust heeft ons deugdzaam hart verlaten.
O thee! o vriendschap! o kalmerend licht!

Straks 't balsemende donker, morgen lopen

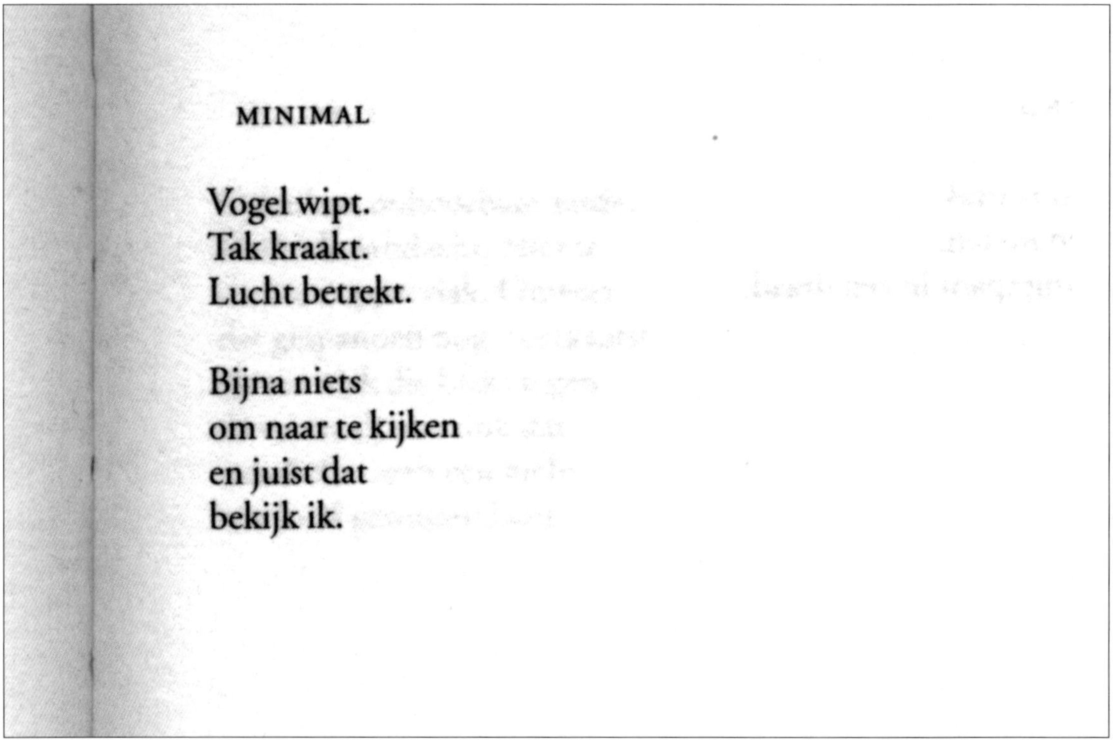

MINIMAL

Vogel wipt.
Tak kraakt.
Lucht betrekt.

Bijna niets
om naar te kijken
en juist dat
bekijk ik.

efficiency efficiëntie

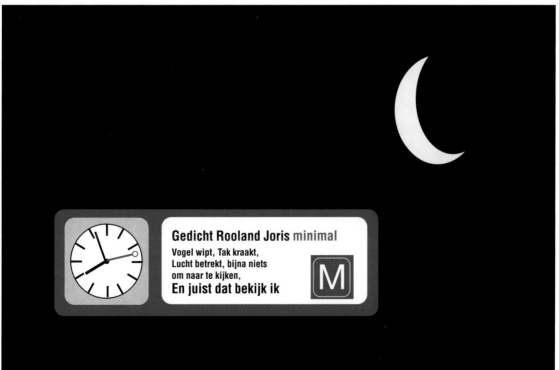

Gedicht Rooland Joris minimal

Vogel wipt, Tak kraakt,
Lucht betrekt, bijna niets
om naar te kijken,
En juist dat bekijk ik

[M]

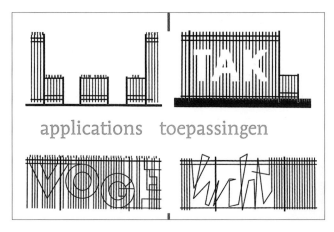

applications   toepassingen

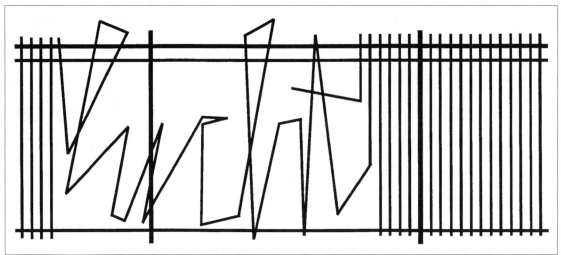

border
grens

PROPOSAL AND COUNTER-PROPOSAL

Theme III

Visual Essay

ANDREAS TETZLAFF

Poetry in Urban Spaces

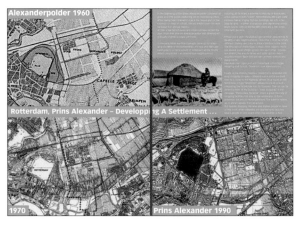

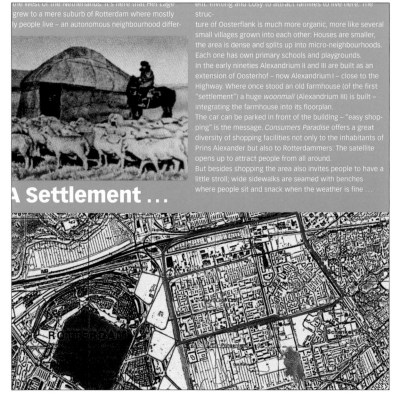

the west of the Netherlands. It's here that *Het Lage* grew to a mere suburb of Rotterdam where mostly ly people live – an autonomous neighbourhood differ-

ent: inviting and cosy to attract families to live here. The struc-

ture of Oosterflank is much more organic, more like several small villages grown into each other: Houses are smaller, the area is dense and splits up into micro-neighbourhoods. Each one has own primary schools and playgrounds.

In the early nineties Alexandrium II and III are built as an extension of Oosterhof – now Alexandrium I – close to the Highway. Where once stood an old farmhouse (of the first "settlement") a huge *woonmall* (Alexandrium III) is built – integrating the farmhouse into its floorplan.

The car can be parked in front of the building – "easy shopping" is the message. *Consumers Paradise* offers a great diversity of shopping facilities not only to the inhabitants of Prins Alexander but also to Rotterdammers: The satellite opens up to attract people from all around.

But besides shopping the area also invites people to have a little stroll; wide sidewalks are seamed with benches where people sit and snack when the weather is fine …

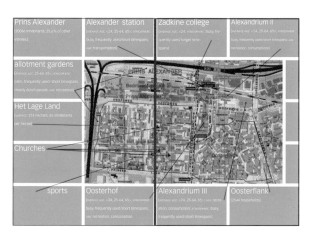

Prins Alexander
(20086 inhabitants; 25,6 % of other ethnies)

Alexander station
[average age: <24, 25-64, 65>; atmosphere: busy, frequently used/short timespans; aim: transportation]

Zadkine college
[average age: <24; atmosphere: busy, frequently used/longer timespans]

Alexandrium II
[average age: <24, 25-64, 65>; atmosphere: busy, frequently used/short timespans; aim: recreation, consumption]

allotment gardens
[average age: 25-64, 65>; atmosphere: calm, frequently used/ short timespans, mostly dutch people; aim: recreation]

Het Lage Land
[surface: 214 hectare; 45 inhabitants per hectar]

Churches

sports

Oosterhof
[average age: <34, 25-64, 65>; atmosphere: busy, frequently used/ short timespans; aim: recreation, consumption]

Alexandrium III
[average age: <24, 25-64, 65>; aim: recreation, consumption; atmosphere: busy, frequently used/short timespans;]

Oosterflank
[2544 households]

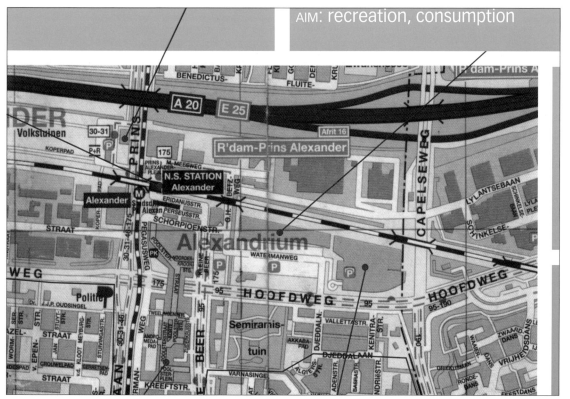

AIM: recreation, consumption

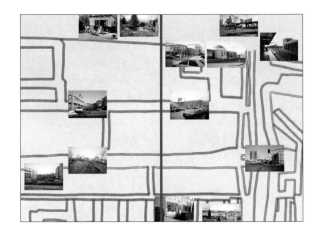

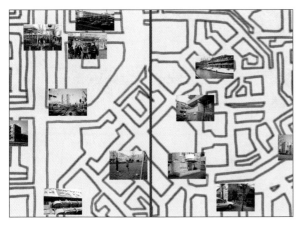

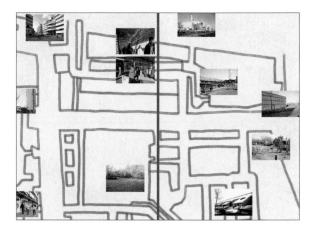

...a poem should be like
a temporary »visitor« at
Alexandrium II...

PROPOSAL AND COUNTER-PROPOSAL
Theme III
Visual Essay
Poetry in Urban Spaces

Designing is a combination of the formation of ideas and of language. During different phases of the Post-St. Joost curriculum, students are repeatedly confronted with different language genres, and this is precisely because the emphasis in undergraduate design education has been focussed more on developing a feeling for image and form. Poetry is one of those forms of language – and presumably the most experimental form – to which a separate project is devoted. By bringing the intimacy of the poet's world into the urban setting, the crossroads between the private and the public are once again explored, but so are the barriers dividing so-called 'high' culture and ordinary culture. Poetry on traffic signs, poetry on the fence around a park. Texts for passing pedestrians. These are messages that do not try to sell anything and which need no reply from those casual passers-by in order to retain their right to exist, as would be the case for highway department signs or lettering affixed to building facades. The setting in which the texts appear in a city is realistic, yet at the same time completely open. No quasi-assignment is being simulated. Instead, the projects are specifically designed for their location.

Poetry in Urban Spaces

'Can a poetic text, once introduced in the urban environment, hold its own amongst, beside and facing the flood of communications and the rigid information systems that government and other institutions have imposed on public space?'
Hugues Boekraad, Annual Report, Post-St.Joost 1999, p. 176

**PROPOSAL AND
COUNTER-PROPOSAL**
Theme III
Visual Essay
**Poetry in Urban Spaces
FLOOR HOUBEN**

proposal for Johan Willem Frisolaan

In the spring rain,
a child's wet ball
sits on a roof.

Buson

Is there a connection between the name of a street and its identity?
I investigate this question by interjecting poems into an existing system of street names.

In the end, five haikus were printed on street signs. They tell of brief moments that should subtly appeal to passers-by.
– The poems were placed in the conventional design and format of the street signs, emphasizing the contrast between the random naming of streets and text that relates to the environment.
– The location also plays an important role. The signs are within a circum-scribed area of a certain street, placed in undefined locations. Where signs are normally at the junction of a sidewalk and grassy areas, now they are inside the grassed area, redefining the way identity is given to a public space.

proposal for Minister Nelissenstraat

A ball came rolling,
up to my feet, my
aimless feet.

Hakussen

proposal for Minister Nelissenstraat

My scissors approached
the white chrysanthemum –
and hesitated.

Buson

proposal for Johan Willem Frisolaan

proposal for Johan Willem Frisolaan

From which tree
came the blossoms? Only
their scent I know.

So many different
difficult names has
the grass of spring.

Basho

Shado

PROPOSAL AND COUNTER-PROPOSAL
Theme III
Visual Essay
Poetry in Urban Spaces
ALAN FITZPATRICK

WHAT A JOY, TO KNOW, EVEN WHEN WE CAN'T SEE
[citizen to soldier]
OR HEAR YOU, THAT YOU ARE AROUND,

THOUGH VERY FEW OF YOU FIND US WORTH
[soldier to citizen]
LOOKING AT, UNLESS WE COME TOO CLOSE.

Excerpt from *Address to the Beasts* by W.H. Auden

In my research for a location in the city of Breda for the Poetry in urban space project I had to first realize that I was observing as a foreigner, comparing Breda to my previous experiences of what a city was. I chose the Kasteelplein as my location because I was interested in how the traditional theme of the military is integrated into a modern city. My research also brought up the broader theme of historical symbolism in the academy itself: the 'moat and drawbridge' as a reassuring physical monument of power and protection to the city's population. To me the Kasteelplein represented a powerful physical symbol of the relationship between a soldier and citizen. Because it is both a secret and partly public location, soldier and citizen may pass each other every day, but rarely meet.
How could I use poetry to bring an awareness of such an intangible phenomenon?

I brought two opposing poems together using two lines from the first poem which could simultaneously act as a physical voice for both soldier and citizen. This was to present two contrasting perspectives. In the application of this text to the physical space I tried to reconcile the two ideologies side by side and show what they had in common as well as placing them directly in opposition. This idea is reinforced by the direction that the text is read which corresponds to which direction you are standing relative to the two academy buildings.
The interaction between the two texts themselves also represents the interaction of soldier and citizen as they walk around the square of the Kasteelplein either coming from the city center or from the Valkenberg park. Does the passer-by choose to walk on top of or in between the larger text? Does he/she walk or march? What is the most commonly walked route around the square?

Above: *The execution was visualized as an application of a paint-like powder which would be worn away by the footsteps of those who walked over it. This would reveal the most often used route through the Kasteelplein. The larger text is from Address to the Beasts. This is interspersed with smaller text from Aubade.*

Top and bottom: *texts taken from two poems by W. H. Auden which are combined for the final design shown on the opposite page.*

YOUR OWN HABITATIONS ARE COSY AND PRIVATE,
NOT PRETENTIOUS TEMPLES.

OF COURSE YOU HAVE TO TAKE LIVES TO KEEP YOUR OWN,
BUT NEVER KILL FOR APPLAUSE.   Excerpt from *Aubade* by W.H. Auden

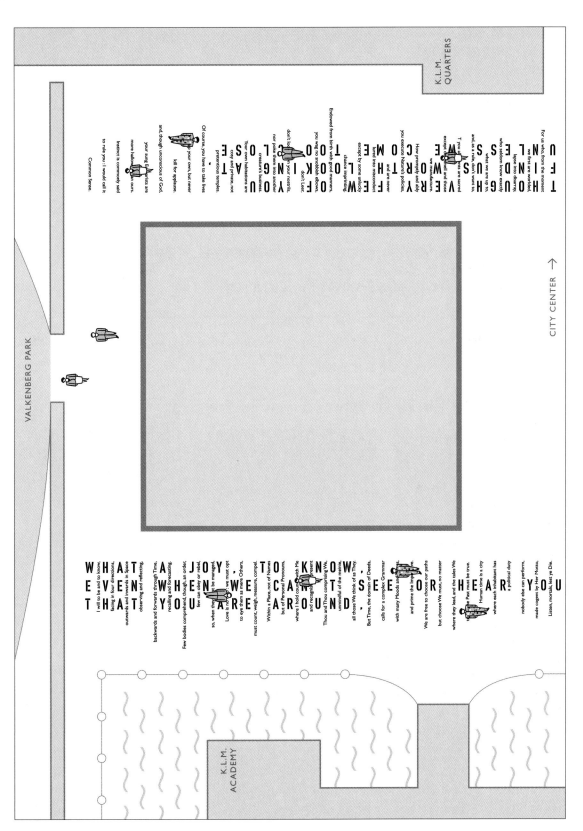

**PROPOSAL AND
COUNTER-PROPOSAL**
Theme III
Visual Essay
Poetry in Urban Spaces
STEFFEN MAAS

above: *two stills from 'Rain', by Joris
Ivens and Mannus Franken (1929)*

*Bird rocks / Branch cracks / Air moves. / Nearly nothing /
To look at / And just that / I look at.*

Roland Jooris: 'Minimal', from The Museum of the Summer (1974)

Valkenberg Park, Breda

above an below: *Permanent installation of the poem, with the author's name in metal letters (identical treatment as the fence).*
- *City of Breda (Departments of Urban Development and Culture)*
- *The Flemmish Poetry Centre, Gent*
- *Edobode Apparatenbouw, Groningen / Jan Hulsebos Oudeschip (montage)*

**Bird rocks / Branch cracks / Air moves. / Nearly nothing /
To look at / And just that / I look at.**

This poem and the way it is integrated casually confronts the passer-by with the non-architectural environment he passes through. Typography and text attract attention to the fence as a divider between the city and the park. Nonetheless, the text is not emphatic in its presence, as the form and colour of the letters mesh seamlessly with the fence. As the poem expresses a classic Romantic theme, the design engages a dialogue with the visitor in a light and modest tone.

Steffen Maas, november 1999

PROPOSAL AND
COUNTER-PROPOSAL
Theme III
Visual Essay
Poetry in Urban Spaces
ANDREAS TETZLAFF

Poetry as a public event

Chosen Area

Shopfront of Alexandrium II – 'consumers' paradise', a fluctuating, 'forum'-like spot. Mostly very busy: People of all cultural and ethnic back-grounds, Residents as well as Rotterdammers, come here to shop or to have 'a day out'.

The Author

'Anez abu Salim, one of the most famous bedouin smugglers and poet of Sinai.

The Poem

It was composed during emprison-ment. It's part of a series of poems addressing clan-members, friends and (smuggling) colleagues. There are replies on them.

O WRITER, RISE AND WRITE SOME PLEASANT WORDS,
WHOSE MEANING'S LIKE A CURE TO ONE THAT'S ILL.

HE SAYS MY POEMS OF RANDOM SCRAPS ARE MADE,
BUT I SAY THEY'RE A PURE SALIMI BLADE.

I HAVE SOME THOUGHTS I'D SAY THAT MAKE ME SIGH:
DON'T TURN TO MEN, BUT ONLY GOD, FOR AID.

OUR ASKING HIM WHO CANNOT HELP WAS VAIN,
AS VAIN AS TELLING WOMEN OF OUR PAINS;

THOUGH MANY TAKE A BOASTER AT HIS WORD,
I HATE THE BOASTS THAT I HAVE LATELY HEARD.

O GIVE ME CAMELS, THEIR CHEST DARK FROM SWEAT,
WITH LIMESTONE MOUNTAINS UP AND BACK BESET;

REINS TAPPING ON THE POMMELS IS ALL YOU HEAR
AND CAMELS, UNTRAINED, FILL YOUR HEART WITH FEAR;

THE GUIDE GETS LOST AMONG MOUNTAINS HIGH,
NIGHT'S DARK, OUR WATER-SKINS ARE TINDER DRY;

BUT WITH THE DAWN WE PASS MT YAHAMIM,
AND ACROSS THE STONY FLATS WE STREAM.

Taken out of the series 'a poet in prison' by 'Anez abu Salim in: Clinton Bailey, *Bedouin Poetry from Sinai and the Negev*, Oxford/New York 1991

A Story of Transport

'Anez abu Salim composes the poem – a fellow inmate writes it down ('Anez is illiterate) – a 'mes-senger' brings it to a travelling merchant (who drives in his truck to all the tribes) – the merchant reads it to bedouins, 3 or 4 times if they wish to memorize it – the poem spreads from mouth to mouth – people react to it and send something back.

Visualization

The poem is 'morphed' from its original arabic version to its europe-an translation – it's transferred from one alphabetical system into the other, changing from generation to generation (like generations of immigrants assimilating to a foreign city). 8 steps within this process are taken out – like filmstills – and shall be used as a 'score' by 8 street-pain-ters. Each of them realises one of the steps on ground, following his/her own aesthetic interpretation concerning colour and style.

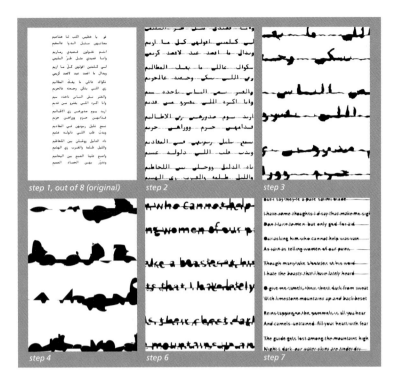

step 1, out of 8 (original)

step 2

step 3

step 4

step 6

step 7

a bedouin poem shouldn't settle – it should happen...

step 5

OPPOSITIONS

H.J.A. HOFLAND
Journalism
MARIJN VAN VILSTEREN
& Rethorics
STEFFEN MAAS

The Murder of the Word When the history of our own time is written, will historians have concluded that we, the generations of the last century, not only inflicted enormous human suffering and material destruction, but even in the process, we perpetrated a murderous assault on our mother tongues? On Dutch, but also on English, German, all the languages of Western civilization? Will it be decided that words can also be destroyed and with them, the concepts for which they stand? Or – an absurd consequence – must the scholars of the future work in, and especially with, the language remnants that we will have left behind, so that they can no longer even fully comprehend what has been lost?

This is the question, it seems to me, that ultimately lies concealed in the projects by Steffen Maas and Marijn van Vilsteren. In an age that prides itself on its 'revolution in communications', day in, day out, we are in the process of making words empty. We deal with words as though they were beasts bred for consumption. We give them additives to make them grow, feed them hormones. We kill the words. We scrape out their innards, remove their organs and their appendages. We spray words with colour dyes and lay them out in display cases. There lie our colossal, synthetic words. They no longer serve to be read. The word, treated for consumption, has become its own advertisement. In its original function, it is dead. It has spoiled and rotted. Now removed from the display case, it is replaced by the next ad that was once the word, and the advertisement for the word has replaced its meaning. Advertising is a step-by-step process, from the enlargement to the surpassing to the exceeding to the ultimately superlative, that highest apex, pinnacle of a top step. May I wish you a very exceptionally incredibly pleasant evening!

Steffen Maas's project includes lettertype. 'Slóbodan Milosevic', from a five-point letter on the first day of the war in Kosovo to more than 35 points on the 67th day. It is the evolution of the war, from concept to outcry, from the reading, in the original sense, to the reaction, to just four-and-a-half letters that remain of a forename. Another segment of the project is comprised of a collection of senseless commonplaces found in politics, advertising and the flash of postmodern industry. What, in God's name, is 'Partners in Young Executive Recruitment'? What is a Partner worth? What is Young? How executive is Executive? Do we read words, or do we see the emptied-out, puffed-up carcasses of words? We see the cadavers; we certainly know that. We smell the wisp of rot, the regular scent in the storm of everyday idle prattle that perpetually zooms over the West.

Marijn van Vilsteren's project came about in New York. The task there, in the capital of the world, is to unravel the paradox. More than anywhere else, it is there, per square foot per minute, that one encounters the largest numbers of cleaned-out carcasses of words, divested of meaning. New York's concentration of word cadavers is greater than in any other place on earth. And yet – this is the paradox – the city works as no other, in both senses of the word, labour and effectiviness. How is this possible? I think it is because the display case words there have a higher speed of rotation than anywhere else in the world. In the postmodern rhetoric, New York has developed a language of its own. This is a language that one has to learn there because it cannot be learned anywhere else. In New York, in order to comprehend, from their point of view, the sum-ming up of words in green italic print in the chapter on 'Who's to Blame?', one has to learn to read all over again. And as a heart-breakingly absurd contradiction, we see the Pope, the Holy Father, bedecked with all the paraphernalia of the earthly representative of God, in the photograph above the caption: 'The Pope Now has a Website.' Certainly. Why wouldn't the Pope have a website? Why wouldn't he eat a Big Mac? Why shouldn't he ride a 1000cc motor-cycle? Who or what is being made into an advertising cadaver, the Pope or the website?

In both of these projects about 'journalism and rhetoric' (politics and advertising, I think, belong here, too), the word is put on view, extricated from its origins. And what matters is that one must have experienced it in order to judge it. In his novel, Hampton Court, Menno ter Braak's protagonist discovers a matchbox. In looking at this little box, which is in no way distinguishable from any other matchbox, he is overwhelmed by the detachment, the event within his brain whereby this box, stripped of its function, is suddenly removed from its surroundings and consequently takes on an absurd presence. A comparable discovery lies at the root of the rediscovery of words, stripped of their meaning, now lying about as preened, dressed, inflated cadavers of words, put on view in the showcase of journalism, of politics, of advertising.

A word has a life. It has its ups and downs. It best presents itself, coincidentally, in a given typography, in a given context. I'll give an example: the word kaput, which assumed worldwide fame in the Second World War and the novel by Curzio Malaparte. I find that it took its most beautiful form in its most poignant meaning on

May 5th, 1945, the day of the German defeat, on the front page of the 'The Maple Leaf', the Canadian army newspaper. 'KAPUT' could not have meant more than it did on that day in that lettertype. All the kaputs ever since are less kaput than this kaput. This is not to say that the word has since become unusable, only that it could never again appear in this beautiful form, and that each misuse of context would subsequently be punished with a further weakening of its significance. Words can only preserve their meaning, and their beauty, if you will, for one is more receptive to it than another, if people do not wring them out and press them into purposes alien to their being. Once exposed to the process of being emptied out and blown up, a word dies and never again returns to its origins.

One of our shortcomings is that we can not remember how we learned to speak. What happens in the brain of a child as he discovers that a certain combination of sounds has a certain meaning, this meaning and no other? In order to be able to remind ourselves, in addition to a good memory, we should as children already have other words at our disposal with which to identify our memory. The spoken word is the oldest form of remote control. The child says, 'Water'. Mother arrives with a glass. In the end we know thousands of words that give us the capacity to 'exchange ideas' in millions of ways. It is a very complicated, always different, form of mutual remote control.

We, having become well-educated speakers in our mother tongue, could better imagine this if we knew no more than a few words in a foreign language, without understanding them in their entire substance – objective meaning, passive meaning, metaphorical function, emotional value. There are Dutch tourists who expand our civilization by teaching our 'dirty' words to the waiters in café terraces overseas. The next fellow countryman, unaware that he is ordering his coffee from such a student, is entertained to a choice selection of triumphantly proclaimed ugly words. Laughter. Linguistically speaking, this is a case of failed remote control. The word has a different function for the user than it does for the receiver.

There is a question that evolves from these projects by Steffen Maas and Marijn van Vilsteren. What are the consequences for verbal remote control if the words are worked into adorned cadavers of words, empty letter combinations whose tour ends at the moment the next appears, the next comparative, the superior, the superlative, now the ultimate and tomorrow yet different again, the super-ultra-supreme rhetoric? With each successive round, distrust of language is on the rise. In their final gift, both of these projects bear witness against those who would make use of the word by killing it.

'The Pope Now has a Website.' Certainly. Why wouldn't the Pope have a website? Why wouldn't he eat a Big Mac? Why shouldn't he ride a 1000cc motorcycle?

H.J.A. HOFLAND

OPPOSITIONS
H.J.A. HOFLAND
Journalism
MARIJN VAN VILSTEREN
& Rethorics
STEFFEN MAAS

Hello Down There (1997) The theme of my book is the way American culture presents and reproduces itself. It was made together with David Beker, a student of American Studies and History at the University of Amsterdam. We tried to sketch an image of American culture, based on the 1996 presidential election campaign.

We wanted to be realistic in terms of our possibilities for realizing such an objective. The only way we could sensibly approach it was to go to the United States in the thought that we needed to confront our presuppositions (from our respective fields) with the huge exposé of Americana offered by the election campaign. A number of subordinate themes quickly crystallized: the conflicting interests of politicians and the public, the influence of business on politics, the impossibility of politicians keeping their promises, the power of the media and the theatricality they engender, the opportunism of politicians towards different interest groups, the frank compromising of the truth and the way voters take that for granted, the importance of the opinion polls, information, history, heroism, morale, religion, family, antecedents and so on. Our position offered us a chance to understand these conditions, which are often so incomprehensible to Europeans. We concluded that Europeans need to be 'indoctrinated' into American rituals.

At a certain point, we found a course book meant to help Americans master these rituals. We have used eight of the chapters from the textbook in our structuring of Hello Down There. The chapter titles are: 'Conversations with God', 'How to Start your own Law Practice', 'How to Thrive in a Not-So Sensitive World', 'What am I Good At?', 'How to get a Good Night's Sleep', 'Would You like to be Able to Do More than just Dial 911'?, 'The Principle of Seduction' and 'How to Deal with Difficult People'.

We could now introduce our secondary themes, one at a time. Somewhat tongue-in-cheek, perhaps, but certainly not judgementally – we were sooner just surprised. We wanted to demonstrate that there are contradictions in the American Dream. For example, how does the politician 'deal with difficult people', and how different is that to the way the average American citizen is meant to do the same thing?

In 1999, my book was shown at the Stedelijk Museum in Amsterdam. For the exhibition, I made a wall-size photograph. It was a visual conclusion, acting as an eye-catcher that would again emphasize the subjective aspect of my research, which was needed outside the context of the art school. 'Who's to Blame?' is one of my texts, taken from a page towards the end of the textbook. The word BLAME, on a T-shirt worn by the person who made the book, is a commentary on the automatism that many people want to implicate as a factor in the power play within American culture, which they hold responsible for the imbalances that dominate relationships.

It is the Americans who are doing this. The entire election campaign is made up of people pointing a finger at each other. 'Who's to blame?' It is the Europeans who do it as they witness the theatrics of election campaign on the other side of the Atlantic from the perspective of their own culture. 'Who's to blame?' It is a designer and a history student from Holland who went to America to have a look. 'I'm to blame?' As a text on that T-shirt, BLAME works as a logo, characteristic of the cretinism of our time. It works both as a word and as an image.

Salesman
e SECOND One
Just Left!

n Come In 3 Sizes
SMALL,
MEDIUM,
and
H MY GOD!

THIS CLOCK WILL
ER BE STOLEN

Who's to Blame?

Immigrants,
Faggots,
Senators,
Neighbors,
Rapists,
Bosses,
Reagan,
The Poor,
Muslims,
Conservatives,
Writers,
Pollsters,

Men,
Junkies,
Russians,
Singers,
Models,
Whites,
Hookers,
Teachers,
Judges,
Voters,
Satan,
Salesmen,

Fetishists,
Babies,
Policemen,
Drivers,
Lovers,
Elisabeth,
Aliens,
Japanese,
Extremists,
God,
Employers,
Rappers,

Journalists,
Guests,
Teenagers,
Slaves,
Freaks,
Soldiers,
Farmers,
Brothers,
Heterosexuals,
Bodyguards,
Homeless,
Tourists,

Soccermoms,
Millionairs,
Killers,
Astronauts,
Queens,
Beggars,
Rockers,
Strangers,
Shrinks,
Liberals,
Lawyers,
Oprah Winfrey,

Sexists,
Victims,
Atheists,
Parents,
Dentists,
Friends,
Ex-wives,
Nazi's,
Cripples,
Dancers,
Fools,
Truckers,

Heartbreakers,
Indians,
Hikers,
The unemployed,
Role models,
Exhibitionists,
Fat people,
Ghosts,
Democrats,
Donators
Dry cleaners,
Adults,

Bitches,
Members,
Plumbers,
Cowards,
Leaders,
Gays,
Reverends,
Blacks,
Perot,
Mothers,
Germans,
Assistants,

Consumers,
Spies,
Owners,
Sinners,
Deafs,
Tits,
Users,
Creators,
Christians,
Nuns,
Executers,
Crooks,

Activists,
Yankees,
Anti-semitists,
Masters,
Republicans,
Comedians,
Psychotics,
Waiters,
Drunks,
Letterman,
Boyfriends,
Foreigners,

Animals,
Mother Fuckers,
Scientists,
Fans,
Thieves,
Women,
The Rich,
Lesbians,
Angels
Directors,
Veterans,
Players,

Girls,
Sergeants,
Terrorists,
Sheriffs,
Heroes,
Clinton,
Nominees,
Dictators,
Crusaders,
Suckers,
Students,
Gangs,

Bush,
Jews,
Popes,
Obituaries,
Statesmen,
Employees,
Suspects,
Hosts,
Bachelors,
Relatives,
Youngsters,
Tycoons,

OPPOSITIONS
H.J.A. HOFLAND
Journalism
MARIJN VAN VILSTEREN
& Rethorics
STEFFEN MAAS

Kosovo (1999) 'We wish to warn you that the following images may be distressing.' With these words, tv-journalist Henny Stoel turned her eyes away from me, towards her monitor off-screen. What follo- wed was footage of several corp- ses from the war, to which our newscaster added that the ima- ges had been taken by amateurs. I alerted my attention to what was to come. As I had been made aware of the possibility of shocking scenes, I looked all the more intently for a detail that might touch me. But they only affected me because they were amateur footage. It did not last long. Henny Stoel immediately followed with a report that the members of the Radio Philharmonic Orchestra were distri- buting a pamphlet, in addition to the regular programme booklet. They had begun playing ten minutes late. Not ten minutes of silence, as I would have expected from musicians, but they had organized a speech to precede their afternoon concert, in support of their demands for a better labour contract.

Henny Stoel has pretty eyes and makes me think of an amiable next-door neighbour. When the news was over, she gave a friendly nod. She was a caricature that you could make a sketch of. I glanced outside, past my television. As a child, I thought, you can only see your mother as your mother, a character. Diagonally across the way, someone was watching a film. An image flickered in the pitch-black room, indistinguishable within the darkness of the street that lie between us. A shiny, artificially lit sportscar drove into our two rooms, to then be cut off by an invisible frame through which it sped away. I wanted to continue working on the pamphlet that was going to be my final project. I decided on ten minutes of silence first. Meanwhile, the chase was on and we were now in hot pursuit, threatening the car from behind. Then a group of nurses in white uniforms rushed through an American hospital with a bed and an IV drip. It looked 'realistic'. I would be able to follow the news reports, or in any case the rest of the war, this way, if my neighbour left his curtains open for the next few days.

For now, I had to look for a couple of phrases from today's newspaper, my daily working materials and a teeming nest of people who talk a lot. When first reading the paper, I had immediately been compelled to circle these crescendos in the requiem that is called Kosovo, painful entities whose typographical enlargements were instantly before my eyes. It was then that I best imagined the essence of the image, in which I had to unite personal emotion, political facts, use

In an age that prides itself on its 'revolution in communications', day in, day out, we are in the process of making words empty.

H.J.A. HOFLAND

of language and graphic solutions, in its most expressive form, because NATO was all too often shooting right past my own objectives, as if a blood-red sportscar were constantly speeding past.

The Third Way *Political and Commercial Use of Language in News on the War in the Balkans.* I began this project because of a general interest in the rhetorical aspects of language and how they are used by the news media. During the process of my work, it appeared that an objective analysis had been superseded by the 'madness of the day'. The events of the past year in Kosovo were very dominant in the media and the not unambiguous reporting, as such, was unavoidable working material. I have combined political statements about the events and various texts from the news media with contemporary commercial recruiting texts that proscribe a 'living and working style', two language registers that do not seem very tolerant of one another. The trendy language, combined with political events, gives insight into journalistic rhetoric, as well as illustrating personal or collective indignation.

selection

opinion

actuality

suggestion

Clockwise from top left:
- *Henri Matisse: 'Through the Wind-Shield' (1917)*
- *Rachel Whiteread: 'Untitled' (1997), (paperbacks)*
- *Mark Manders: 'BLACK BIRD / DEAD BIRD / CURRENT THOUGHT'*
- *The former Chilean dictator, Augusto Pinochet, just before his arrest in 1998*

above left: *Rembrandt:
'De Staalmeesters' (1662), verifying
the books at a town meeting;*
above right: *American judges in
council, newspaper photo during
the Bill Clinton / Monica Lewinsky
scandal (1999)*

left: *'Gerrit-Jan Wolffensperger
stops to let Frits Bolkenstein pass.'*
right: *From an advertisement for
KUB Tilburg*

Prins Charles lijkt, van een afstand
gezien, onaanraakbaar. In de cirkel
rondom hem regeert het niets. Zijn
oogopslag is neutraal, of hij nu zijn
blik gericht houdt op een
folkloristische meisjesdansgroep in
Zuid-Afrika of op een schaal blozende,
ecologisch gekweekte tomaten. Wat
gaat er om achter dat voorhoofd van
de Britse troonopvolger, die vandaag
zijn 50ste verjaardag viert.

Tóch ís Augústo Pinochét président

zomer (Het thema was weggezakt door de vakantie en de algehele Pinochet-moeheid)

■ OH, OH, SANTIAGO

Het is een ándere Pinochet die deze dagen het orginanieuws is in Chili. Robinson Pinochet is arts. Hij schóót zonder aanleiding z'n buurman,

diens echtgenote en één van hun kinderen dóód.

Colo Colo
• De zonderlinge moordenaar houdt de Chilenen bezig. En natuurlijk de wedstrijd vanavond van Colo Colo, de favoriete voetbalclub die tegen Peru speelt om de Beker der Bevrijders.

DE KERK, IN DIT ZÉÉR KATHOLIEKE LAND VAN GRÓÓT

GEWICHT, DENKT NA OVER EEN VERKLARING.

In Santiago hebben **Penochetistas** met hernieuwde energie hun claxóncoñcerten hervat voor de met eieren bekogelde Spaanse ambassade in het stadsdeel ¡Las Condes!

LIBÉRATION: "De duitsers kwalificeren onze president als een negerkoning"

SCHRÖDER ZAHLMEISTER EUROPAS:

Köhl

SCHRÖDER NEEMT WÓÓRDEN IN DE MOND, was in zijn tijd bereid Europese tonont (die zijn voorganger nooit zou hebben gebruikt) moetingen op het laatste moment te redden "HET GOEDE DUITSE GELD WORDT IN BRUSSEL ERDOOR GEJAAGD"

"met een zak, Duits geld"

"MÉÉR GERECHTIGHEID"

huidige Duitse netto bijdrage: 22 miljard mark

1999 ROTTERDAM
ÖCALAN
ACÄLÓN
AçÖLAN
ÜCÜLÜN
NALACÖ
ZESTIENHOVEN AIRPORT

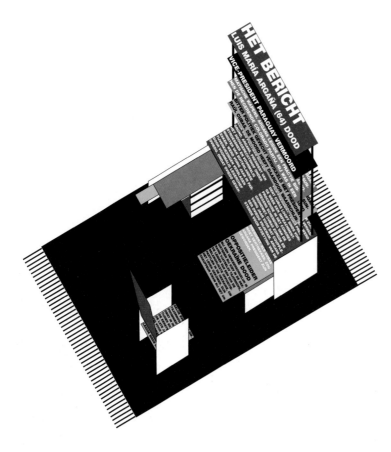

left: *Viennese Modernism*
(Friedl Dicker and Franz Singer
below: Desk for the home of
Dr. Reisner, Vienna (1929)

'My body is only free of all things imaginary when it enters its working space. Everywhere this space is the same, carefully arranged for the pleasures of painting, of writing, of classifying.'
Roland Barthes by Roland Barthes
(1991)

TEHERAN/ BONN, 12 APRIL. De Iraanse president, Mohammed Khatami, heeft gisteren een uitnodiging van de Duitse bondskanselier Gerhard Schröder voor een bezoek aan Duitsland geaccepteerd. Dat is in Teheran en Bonn meegedeeld. Khatami zal "op een geschikt moment" gaan. de uitnodiging werd zaterdag overgebracht door de chef van de Duitse kanselarij, Bodo Hombach. Hombachs bezoek aan Teheran volgde onmiddelijk op de vrijlating van de Duitse zakenman Helmut Hofer, die ter dood was veroordeeld wegens een sexuele verhouding met een Iraanse studente. De kwestie Hofer stond een normalisering van de Duits-Iraanse betrekkingen in de weg. Khatami bracht vorige maand een bezoek aan Italië. (AFP)

DJIBOUTI, 12 APRIL. De presidentsverkiezingen in Djibouti, een stadstaat aan het uiteinde van de Rode Zee, zijn zoals algemeen werd verwacht gewonnen door de kandidaat van de regerende alliantie, Ismail Omar Guelleh (52), die al geruime tijd als sterke man van het regime wordt beschouwd. Volgens de verkiezingscommissie kreeg Omar 74 procent van de stemmen bij een opkomst van 60 procent. de oppositie spreekt van massale stemfraude. omar volgt Hassan Goulad Aptidon (83) op, die aan de macht is geweest sinds de onafhankelijkheid van Frankrijk in 1977. de regering van de nieuwe president erft een zeer slechte economische toestand die zich onder andere uit in chronisch onvermogen de ambtenaren op tijd te betalen en voldoende stroom te leveren. (Reuters, AFP)

GROZNY, 12 APRIL. De president van Tsjetsjenië, Aslan Maschadov, is zaterdag voor de tweede keer in drie weken aan een moordaanslag ontsnapt. In een dorp ten zuiden van de hoofdstad Grozny werd een bom aangetroffen langs de route die de president kort daarop zou nemen voor een toespraak tot aanhangers in het dorp De bom werd onschadelijk gemaakt. Op 21 maart ontkwam Maschadov op het nippertje aan de dood toen een op afstand bediende bom explodeerde op het moment waarop hij langsreed. De president is verwikkeld in een felle machtsstrijd met militieleiders die verantwoordelijk zijn voor het klimaat van wetteloosheid in Tsjetsjenië. Zij zijn uit op zijn val, met het argument dat hij te toegeeflijk is in de relaties met Rusland en dat hij weigert van Tsjetsjenië een islamitische staat te maken. (Reuters)

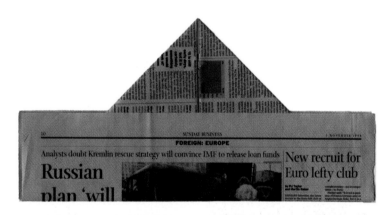

A NEW SENSATION!	A NEW SENSATION!	A NEW SENSATION!
MARTINOVIC	ARKAN	ASSAD
DRASKOVIC	TARKAN	BAGDAD
MILOSEVIC	RADOVAN	NOVISAD
KARADZIC	SLOBODAN	ISLAMABAD
TADIC	BALKAN	BELGRAD
MOSZKOVIC	KOFI ANAN	SIMBAD

'On he went, then, but it was a long way. This road, the village high street, did not in fact lead to Castle Hill, it only went close to it, but then curved away, as if on purpose, and although it took one no farther from the castle, nor did it come any nearer. K. constantly expected the road to turn in the direction of the castle at last, surely it would, and it was only because he expected it that he kept going; obviously, given his weariness, he was reluctant to leave the road, he was also surprised at how long the village was, it went on and on, nothing but tiny houses and iced-up windowpanes and snow and nobody around - finally he tore himself loose from the grip of the high street, a narrow lane swallowed him up, even deeper snow, his feet sank in, it was hard work extracting them, he began to perspire, abruptly he came to a halt and could go no farther.'

Franz Kafka: The Castle, (1997), Penguin Books, a new translation, by J.A. Underwood

The Voice of Freedom IT'S A DIRTY WAR!

The Standard IT IS ALWAYS WAR!

The Euro IT IS NEVER WAR!

DE BEWEGING:
HET IS IMMERS OORLOG!

The Movement — IT IS WAR THOUGH!

DE ZWEEP:
HET IS ALWEER OORLOG!

The Whip — IT IS WAR, AGAIN!

DE WAARHEID:
HET IS BIJNA OORLOG!

The Truth — IT IS NEARLY WAR!

DE ECHO:
HET IS BIJNA VREDE!

The Echo — IT IS NEARLY PEACE!

HET SIGNAAL:
'T WAS METEEN OORLOG!

The Signal — IT WAS WAR RIGHT AWAY!

L'INTERNAZIONALE:
HET IS OVERAL OORLOG!

L'Internazionale — IT IS WAR EVERYWHERE!

HET VOLK:
HET IS BURGER OORLOG!

The People — IT IS A CIVIL WAR!

HET NIEUWS VAN DE DAG
HET IS VANDAAG OORLOG!

The Daily News — TODAY, IT IS WAR!

HET LIBERALE WEEKBLAD
'T IS 'N PROPAGANDA OORLOG!

The Liberal — IT IS A PROPAGANDA WAR!

Welk dieptepunt wilt u terug-zien op een postzegel?

Wij zorgen ervoor.

Leuker kunnen we het niet maken, wel makkelijker.

De BV Nederland.

Vrijheid

VS bieden goede Europeanen iets onbetaalbaars.

Deadlines missen is één ding, een oorlog missen iets anders.

Ideas People Technologies

Power geven aan Partnership.

AlliedForce

Sneuvel-Bereidheid.

Voor wie all-risk te duur vindt.

Misschien hadden we de KorteKlapMethode moeten gebruiken.

NachtVanWiegel.

KannoneerBoot-Politiek

Goed genoeg voor een half miljoen mensen.

'The bourgeois can read and play the piano, all of that. Therefore, because they can all do it just the same way, because they are what they call civilized people, that is why we dislike them so much. That is we are so happy to listen to the crudeness and the vulgarity of lesser folk. It is obvious that we are not going to help teach them to read and play the piano, because for us, the world would no longer be bearable.'

Lodewijk van Deyssel, ca. 1890

Join us. Together we can change the world.

AlliedForce

De mens lijdt het meest van het lijden dat hij vreest.

Creators of Solutions.

Knuffels uit Kosovo.

Hoe ver het ook is, het is altijd dichtbij.

Laat u zich verrassen of heeft u een scenario?

Partners in Young Executive Recruitment.

Midlife-crisis op je vijftigste?

Wij zetten onze aanvallen onverminderd voort.

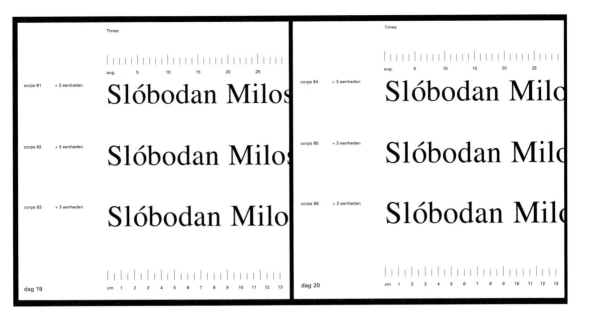

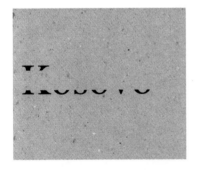

With social phenomena, one has to do not only with the relationships between the individual and the group, or between groups, but also with the fact that these relationships can have a certain semantic meaning and pragmatic effect. (...) Linguistic communication is not usually a neutral reporting of conditions in the world, but envisions influencing another's preferences and behaviour. (...) This has consequences for constructing models. It implies that one must take account of phenomena that (with the exception of biology) do not take place in natural science. (...) The nature of the social phenomenon that one is investigating provides good criteria for dividing social models into two major groups. If one defines 'social' as 'communicative', then one can distingish:

I   models for the structure of communications networks or structural models, and

II models for the rules of the communication (syntactic/semantic/pragmatic rules).

K. Bertels, D. Nauta: Introduction to the Understanding of Models (1974).

Antwerp, late November '99

Hey Steffen! Here is part of the 'Occupied City' by Paul van Ostaijen. But not all of it! That's because my wallet is empty. But it will fill up again and I'll send you the rest. It's a lot. I hope this is what you meant, because I am not quite sure. It is poorly copied, as well. But Best Wishes. For 2000, too! Then I'll be in Malmö, in southern Sweden. Around the first of January, I mean. So I wish you a glorious party and great fireworks. I have also copied 1 page from a book by Daniil Charms. It may be interesting as far as the typography is concerned. But Russians are interesting no matter how you look at it. Are you familiar with Daniil Ch? He is an absolute hero, in my eyes. Take care of yourself!

Charlotte K.

Hoe ver het ook is, het is altijd dichtbij.

However far away, it is always close by.

OPPOSITIONS

A.J.A. VAN ZOEST

Index

MINKE THEMANS

& Meaning

SANDRA OOM

Index and Meaning How does a city let you know it is a city? With its asphalt and its pavements, the noisy traffic, the busses, tramways, automobiles, scooters and bikes? With its high skyline, the clouds just above? By the streams of people moving along the shop windows – everywhere a fellow being out shopping for something, carrying his bounty in a bulging plastic bag? Yes, a city gives out signs of its own: here you are in the city. A museum also sends out its signals. They include the barriers, sometimes very apparent and sometimes barely perceptible, that have been placed between the museum visitors and the objects on exhibition, the border dividing the bidden and the forbidden, between having to look and not being allowed to touch. This is also a division between desire and having something for yourself. Separate galleries, lines on the floor, cameras, guards. Signs that set boundaries are telling us, 'this is a museum – where you should be doing this, but that is not allowed'.

Minke Themans embarked on an investigation of the city, Sandra Oom on a study of the museum. Their basic principles were similar. Each recorded how people experienced the object of their research. Their results are not similar, yet they do have something remarkable in common: both are extremely original, both a result of a shift in the way their selected subjects are usually approached.

An investigation is original because someone has looked differently at something. Where the city is concerned, a considerable step is undertaken in one's thinking when that investigation is not seen simply in visual terms, but the other senses are also allowed to have their say. A city is not just seen, it is certainly also heard and smelled, and for the persistent, perhaps even tasted and felt. There are sounds and smells. The observer can perceive them, indeed even take tallies and measurements, but how does one tell about them, report on them? This, the form, was the challenge in a study of the singularity of a Rotterdam street, the Bergweg, a synecdoche for the life of the big city. The innovativeness of this study of the city lies in this, that an example is given for a different means of recording things. Minke Themans' description of the city goes beyond the maquette that indicates the scale of the streets.

A new way of defining the problem can also make a research project original. What are they all about, those barriers in museums that separate the observer from the observed? Once again, how do you relate your findings? In Sandra Oom's presentation, not a sliver is left of what anyone's wildest dreams might have expected. She offers us a catalogue, but what a catalogue it is – and you might also ask, a catalogue for what? It is a museum in book form, with a tension between the pages and the volume of the whole, making the tension between the flat surface and the space, between the two-dimensional and three-dimensional, tangible, palpable. The pages are flat, but the book takes up space, and this is a reference to what happens in a museum. Three-dimensional objects are often exhibited in frontal fashion, as if they were flat. One dimension is left hanging somewhere back behind the wallpaper.

In a double sense, both Sandra Oom and Minke Themans have tackled a problem of representation. Sandra Oom looks at the signs in the museum, signs that say, 'Don't touch me'. In order to observe the situation from this perspective, she removes the work of art from its traditional central role and puts the museum visitor in its place. Look at the way he is standing, how she sits, how he walks, what he is experiencing. Minke Themans, in her turn, puts the city in the spotlight: city, show us who you are. Having reflected on that, after their observations, both researchers set themselves the task of giving the most highly individualistic representations possible of those representations.

Representation is a moment in a process of giving something meaning. Take a photograph of a pile of cigarette butts. It represents a pile of cigarette butts, a representation that gives the viewer little difficulty in making the link to what is being represented. The sign, or symbol, is a visualized signal. There is a kinship in the appearance of the image and what is (re)presented by that image. In the reality of our lives, however, a pile of cigarette butts dumped in the street represents something else in its own turn. Someone who sees it also sees the driver who opened his car window and just dumped out his ashtray. Easy. Inconsiderate. No regard for anyone else. This automobile owner is the young distant cousin in the family of those soiling the environment, the same family the big boys belong to, the operators of ruptured oil tankers, the chemical factories that left the Dutch Volgermeer Polder soaked in dioxin. Signs or symbols in which such relationships as these are drawn (in time, in space) are signs of contiguity, of proximity. There is also a third manner of representation, one that depends on mutual agreement. In traffic, for example, there are conventions, codes that determine that 'red' is associated with 'no', a triangle not without its pitfalls. Signs of language, be they letters, words or sentence constructions, are in principle, codified signals. The language is the code.

The American logician and philosopher, Charles Sanders Pierce (1839-1914), who defined the three forms, called the visual image the icon, the contiguous image the index and the image by agreement the symbol. Of these three, the icon fulfils its seductive task primarily in art and poetry, and also in the work of designers, who continue to be practising artists and poets. The symbol does its work wherever communication at the consensus level is required, the level of 'reasonableness'. The index is the finger pointed at a tangible reality.

Representation is but one moment in how something acquires meaning in the semiotic process. Meaning happens when someone immediately, without circumlocution, puts an interpretation to it. Giving meaning, 'semiosis', is that game of representation and interpretation. The character functions when it indicates something and ignites that light in someone's mind. When I hear someone mutter, 'the filthy slob', as he steps over the pile of cigarette stubs, I know that a semiotic connection has been made.

No symbol is pure icon, pure index or pure symbol. There is something of the icon in the conventional use of the colour red to indicate forbidden territory. There is conventionality in pictograms. We all understand that we must walk straight ahead, and not upwards, when the arrow indicating the exit points heavenwards. Roughly speaking, that pictogram is an icon, but one that only has a semiotic function by the grace of convention (vertical arrow means go straight). When Minke Themans wants to indicate the size of a surface, she can make use of convention with multiples of football fields, which she then systematically depicts in small format. In other words, the football fields are represented in icon form. To indicate passageways from gallery to gallery, in a context of her own making, Sandra Oom can make use of our ingrained habit of reading three dimensions into lines on a two-dimensional surface. Automatically, our brain opens up the two-dimensional presentation into a spatial one: habit slides a convention under the icon.

The contiguity of the index is sometimes obvious. Smoke in the distance? There's a fire. A footprint in the sand? The island is inhabited. Sometimes you have to think a little more about it. A photograph of houses with ladders leaning against them, accessing the upstairs apartments – what is that an index for? You imagine some situation where the tenants have to climb up the ladders to reach their rooms. When Pierce wanted to explain what he meant by index signs, he said, 'Everything that strikes us, that touches us, is an index.' An index is everything that commands our attention. This is very true. Of all the different signs and symbols, it is the index that most possesses this power: we are affected by it. Whenever our hearts are affected, and index is at work. The meaning may indeed not be immediately clear. The interpretation can certainly also be completely mistaken. You hear a huge rumble. A bomb? War? Thunder? Some idiot setting off fireworks? The thunderous bang is a sign. We need only to find out what the sign is of. Even the most minimal of indices can be an oeuvre ouvert, a sign with a multitude of interpretations. Much depends on the context and the semiotic capabilities of the person doing the interpreting.

Then too, signs are like living beings, subject to the workings of time. They live and they die. Indices vanish and make way for new indices. Pierce gave a 'street cry' as an example of an index. That was in 1902. At the time, tradesmen announced themselves by calling out in the streets. As a child, in the 1930s, I could hear them moving through the streets, the milkman, the potato wagon, the coal cart, the man with the Berlin sausage buns and the rag man with his hand cart and his enigmatic chant, 'Rags and bones, rags and bones!' Friday was a happy day, because Klaas always appeared, the jolly fishmonger from Volendam, with his broad trousers and his cry of 'tasty sole and fresh eel!' These aural street indices have been chased away, voted out of existence. That fact makes us aware of how mobile and how transitory human semiotic activity is.

In the theoretical sense, the investigations of the Post-St. Joost researchers are important in that they all present a new model for description. Together with that obvious theoretical component, the fact that they are bound by time – they record the indices from the city of today, from the museum of today – gives them a somewhat less self-evident historical aspect. This is made more explicit in the photograph of a segment of a wall, where we read the following:

'THE FIRST STONE LAID ON 16 JUNE, 1884, by Petronella Hendrika Cornelia de Groot, aged 15.'

A nostalgic index. The girl who once stood there would be 131 years old this year. Not only the date, but also her old-fashioned, very Dutch name brings us back to a time when the urban indices of the Bergweg were completely different to those of today. For a grandfather, the first stone is an index of a by-gone world, but a contemporary passer-by just thinks, 'Oh, they were still doing that back then.' The photograph in Minke Theman's book gives the Bergweg an age, adds an historic dimension, a quick craquelure opening up the surface of its world.

The French poet, Paul Eluard, entitled one of his collections, Donner à voir. The title was a programme. The poetry made it possible for readers to notice something that they would probably otherwise not notice. Researchers are like poets. They give the world depth and meaning. In the street, I will from now on take a serious sniff of the steaming souvenir of a passing dog and think, 'an index of the city'. In the museum, from a considerable distance I will henceforward recognize that braided velvet cord looped between the arms of a chair in which I would so gladly have rested my weary self. The barrier. Sitting down is forbidden. This is an index, and I know its meaning.

I will from now on take
a serious sniff of the steaming
souvenir of a passing dog and
think, 'an index of the city'.

A.J.A. VAN ZOEST

OPPOSITIONS
A.J.A. VAN ZOEST
Index
MINKE THEMANS
& Meaning
SANDRA OOM

The Bergweg (1999) A New System of Notation for Urban Situations The city is a space pinned with labels. Pre-programmed, we move through its streets with ease and as a consequence, the way the city itself works seems to have lost importance. We orientate ourselves the same way machines do. For its user/resident, as a visual system and as an urban machine, the city is a single entity. In my project, the visual culture and inner workings of the city are unravelled in a case study of a single street, the Bergweg in North Rotterdam. As a former resident, I am familiar with the street, but without really having known it, which makes it an interesting subject for study. Moreover, there are many of the visual and functional aspects of urbanization evident in the Bergweg, the one that most quickly springs to mind being its role as a through route into the centre of Rotterdam.

A street can be visualized cartographically (a street map), demographically (charts and tables) and photographically (a photo album). This project adds another element to the list, with an 'info-graphic' dimension. Use is made of existing systems of notation or visualization in order to represent functional aspects and statistical data, for example, how long, how wide and how high the Bergweg is, how far the smell of dog faeces travels, and so on. These are combined in new ways, so that statistics are also communicated on a conceptual and emotional level. By using a football field, an airplane and, for instance, the Eiffel Tower, quantitative data about the street become something we can envision.

The form that the appearance of the street takes does not lend itself to a few quantitative facts, however interesting these may be. If one takes the point of view of its inhabitants, then it is precisely the qualitative facts that matter to his or her senses. In this project, relevant quantitative aspects are combined with qualitative features and developed into new forms for recording and visualizing information. By means of tallies, measurements, sketches, pictograms, diagrams, figurative analyses and atmospheric images, I describe the physical, invisible and also the abstract reality of the Bergweg.

All these different analyses and notations are collected in a single book, which can be seen as the visual equivalent of a literary essay about the contemporary street – or city. The book is being published in the year 2000, by 010 Publishers. This prepublication sample shows a selection of the notations it includes.

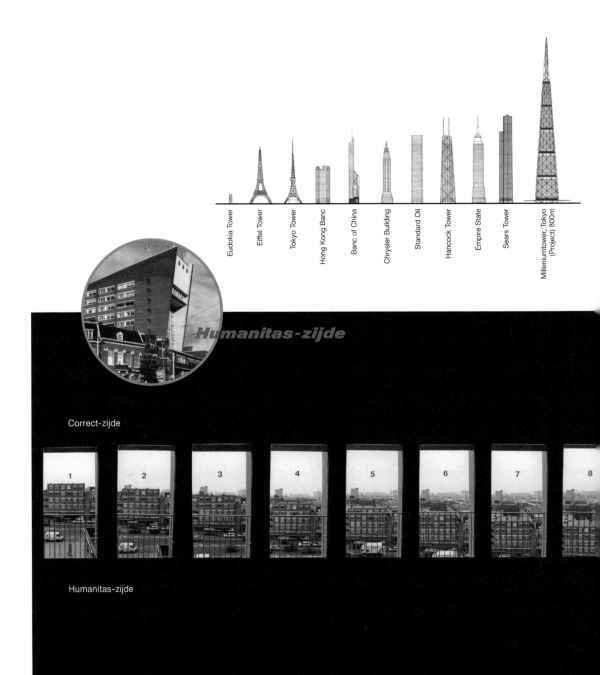

Eudokia Tower

Eiffel Tower

Tokyo Tower

Hong Kong Banc

Banc of China

Chrysler Building

Standard Oil

Hancock Tower

Empire State

Sears Tower

Milleniumtower, Tokyo
(Project) 800m

Humanitas-zijde

Correct-zijde

Humanitas-zijde

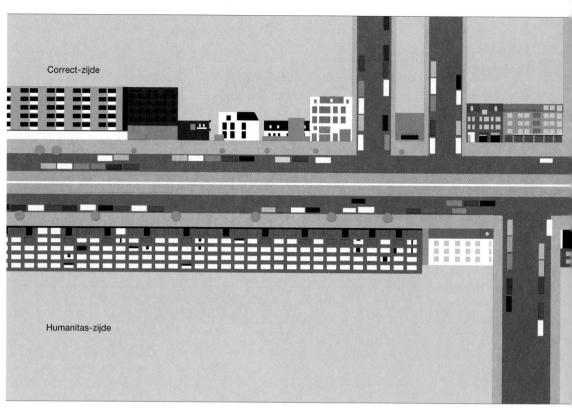

Correct-zijde

Humanitas-zijde

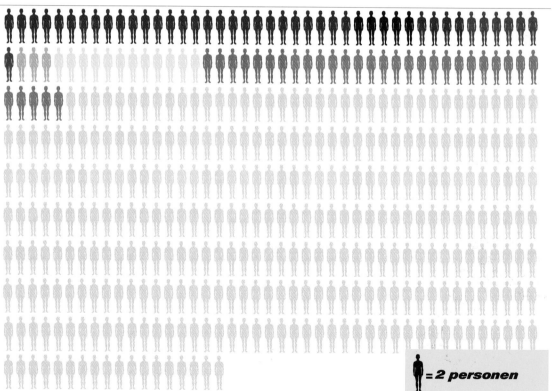

= 2 personen

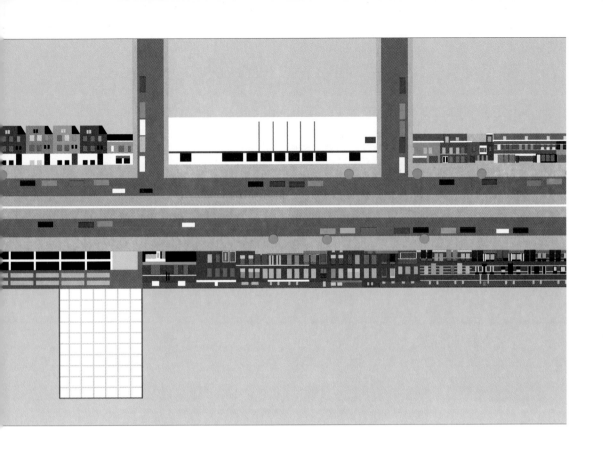

fietsenrekboom
10%

reclameboom
5%

conversatieboom
5%

vuilnisboom
45%

hondenpoepboom
35%

beschermdeboom
35%

Humanitas-zijde

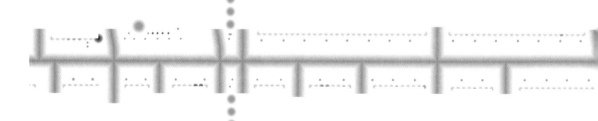

Correct-zijde

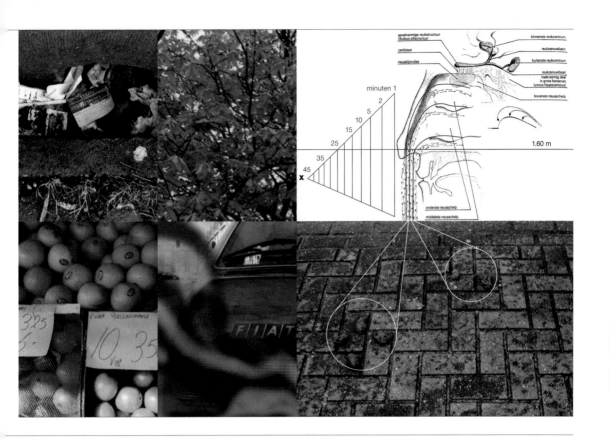

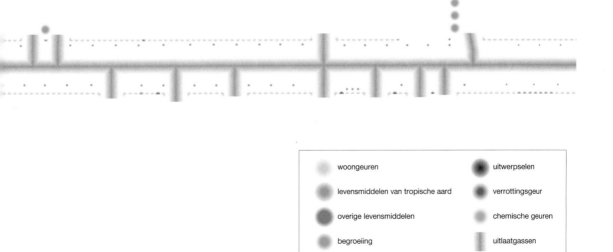

woongeuren		uitwerpselen	
levensmiddelen van tropische aard		verrottingsgeur	
overige levensmiddelen		chemische geuren	
begroeiing		uitlaatgassen	

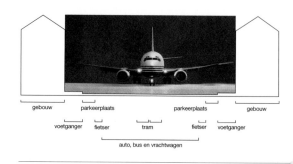

gebouw · parkeerplaats · parkeerplaats · gebouw

voetganger · fietser · tram · fietser · voetganger

auto, bus en vrachtwagen

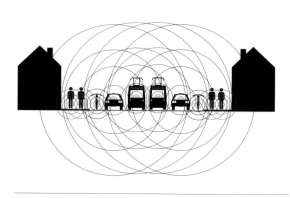

Humanitas-zijde

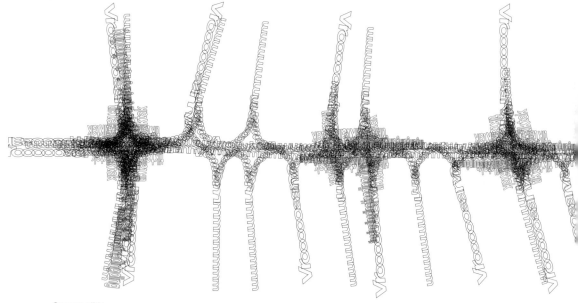

Correct-zijde

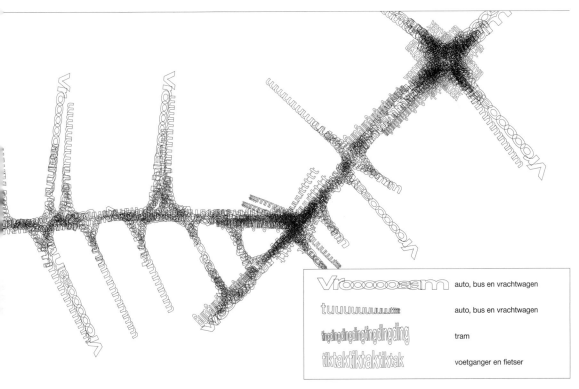

Vroooooaaaim	auto, bus en vrachtwagen
tuuuuuuuuutttt	auto, bus en vrachtwagen
tingdingdingdingtingdingding	tram
tiktaktiktaktiktak	voetganger en fietser

Humanitas-zijde

Correct-zijde

de Bergweg

new systems of notation for urban situations

nieuwe notatiesystemen voor stedelijke situaties

Museum (1998) When I walk around a museum, I notice that as I do, my experience of the objects on display is guided by either visible or invisible barriers. Within this defined space, my behaviour is being subjected to rules. After a certain point, this becomes a hindrance. The regulations are not there to aid understanding, but to protect. The objects themselves have been put on exhibition in such a way that the only connection with them is visual, with any other kind of contact made difficult or prevented altogether. The (in)visible barriers keep communicating the same information: 'do not touch me, keep your distance, do not get a grip on me'. This effect is reinforced by the arrangement of the objects, which for the most part are displayed only frontally. The vehicle of presentation – display case, pedestal, frame – has a single function, as a physical support for the objects, giving no support to the specific way we experience something unique. They seem to be part of a system that reveals itself in the way museums numbers their objects. They are counted just the way we visitors are counted. This system comes between me and the objects being shown.

My project: a 'museum' that encompasses two investigations.
In my first study, I focussed on the interrelationships between the museum objects and the visitors. The means of presentation I identified are visualized as points, lines and planes within a system of demarcation, which is itself kept in the background. Fire alarms, guards and electrical outlets are also part of the defensive system of barriers. The safe, aesthetic space of the museum would appear to be a machine for disciplining its visitors, silently affecting their behaviour. Objects on exhibition are translated as abstract forms, trapped in a system of regulations made visible here. I have selected the book form as my medium, one with two aspects that I have made use of. As an object, a book has three dimensions, and it can therefore serve as a miniaturized model for an architectural space. Secondly, the two-dimensional medium of a book's typographical space has also been employed. A small selection is presented from a series of 30 books. In order to emphasize the artificiality of the museum regulatory system I illustrate, I make use of the traditional idiom of the monumental exhibition.

This brings me to my second study, which concerns the prescribed functions of the vehicles of presentation generally utilized by museums. Despite the introduction of contemporary presentation techniques and media, the detachment and frontality which I observed generally still

Galleries, stripes on the floor, cameras, guards. The museum also demarcates the border between wanting and having.

A.J.A. VAN ZOEST

determine the relationship between the visitor and the display object. I attempt to reverse that relationship, so that it is no longer the object that is the self-evident focal point of the exhibition, but the visitor. As a result, the central point of the exhibition consequently becomes more mobile. The exhibition literally moves.

Inv. nr. 00.151.
The function of each object is
written on a small card.

Inv. nr. 00.161.
The obvious subject of the
exhibition is not the object,
but the visitor.

Inv. nr. 00.177.
Wallpaper for Museums. The desired
number of visitors per m². Available
in three versions.

Inv. nr. 00.160.
The museum system is revealed
in the numbering of the objects.
They are numbered just the way
the visitors are.

Inv. nr. 00.180.
This catalogue is an autonomous
object. It contains inventory
numbers 00.101 through 00.180.

» museum*

museum*

> vervolg museum*

Inv. nr. 00.117. Inv. nr. 00.118. Inv. nr. 00.119.

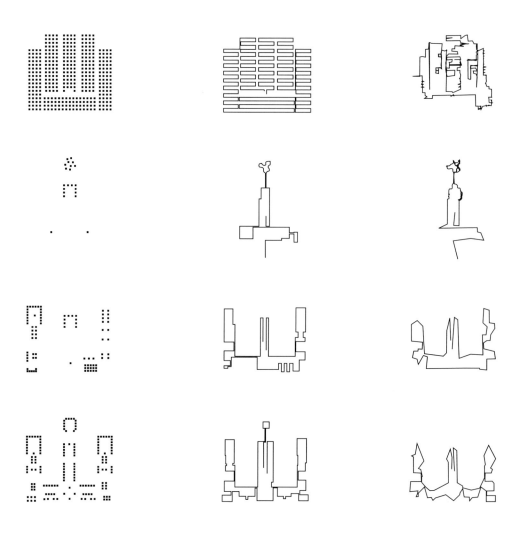

As an object, the book has three
dimensions and is a scale model
for an architectural space.

Inv. nr. 00.117
Positions of the means of presen-
tation and the objects on exhibition.
Dimensions:15 x 15 x 15cm

Inv. nr. 00.118
The usual route followed in a
museum. Dimensions: 7 x 10 x 2cm

Inv. nr. 00.119.
The route of a abritrary visitor
Dimensions: 7 x 10 x 2 cm.

Basement

Ground floor

1st floor

2nd floor

3rd floor

OPPOSITIONS
DIRK VAN WEELDEN
Poetry
BARBARA DIJKHUIS
& Product
JANJAAP RIJPKEMA

The Sleepwalker They say I look like Luc Nilis. Perhaps others enjoy hearing something like that. I do not. It is a handicap. Nothing against Nilis, by the way, but if there is something I don't need, it is that people see me as somebody famous. In order to complete my mission in life, I must not attract attention, you could say, be invisible. I have already been waiting for the blast for so long. The real one, the one that only appears when the explosion is so huge and so beautiful that you forget what went into the air. A burning blossom that surpasses the bloom.

I was with my neighbour, Homo Henk, Homo Henk because I have a brother-in-law whose name is also Henk, but he's not a homo. That Henk is my sister's pimp and I would only go to a film with him if he had the lead, as the prisoner of a serial killer who casually and unfalteringly hangs him up in a sound-proof cellar and every day, day after day, peels away another layer of his skin. Then the murderer takes out a pot full of blue-green flies, specially cultivated for our hero, that swarm out from the jam jar like a squadron of buzzing Japanese Zeros straight out of W-W-2. Then he patiently shoots a video of the creatures fattening up on Henk's raw flesh and laying their eggs in it. During the interval, Henk has to stay in his seat while I go get him a beer and a hot dog.

Homo Henk said he thought the special effects of our film were fantastic, especially the final scene where the last policeman, a silent Indian type, launched himself on a motorcycle. He hurtles at breakneck speed towards a kind of ski jump onto a building site where the gangsters are about to take off in a helicopter. The Indian flies into the air, shooting all the while, and rams into the rising helicopter. It, of course, bursts into bits. Full tank of fuel, big orange fireball. Everybody is dead, except the love of the next-to-the-last dead cop, who stumbles away with her hands covering her mouth. She is still wearing her see-through nurse's uniform: they had picked her up at the hospital where she works. H.H. asks if I think the nurse is tasty. I shrug my shoulders. It's okay, Homo Henk, it's okay.

He most appreciates the Indian cop's suicide mission. And the close-up shots of the exploding chopper. They'd done a good editing job. It lasted for twenty seconds or so, with a lot of slow motion. And that heavy digital sound, which is why I go to that particular theatre. Homo Henk struts out, shaking his head. Damned if it wasn't like feeling the heat of the blow right there, man, in your face, he says.

I think he got off most on the sentimental effect of the good-looking Indian who silently barbecued himself to wipe out the bad guys.

The film had left me quiet – so had the Indian, by the way – but because I was reminded that mine could not be a kamikaze mission. I want to feel the thrill of lots of orange fireballs in my face, but walk away in one piece. Not stumble off like the pretty little nurse, not run away like somebody with something to escape from, but sauntering. I must become a full-fledged sleepwalker, and as far as I am concerned, not a thing of it needs to be put on film. Preferably not.

I have useful information, off the internet, about Timothy McVeigh, the idiot who blew up that government building in Oklahoma City. Typical, a retarded redneck who thinks it is government that is waging war on the people. But that fertilizer bomb of his was powerful and cheap to make. Add a tank of gas and it produces exactly the sort of fireball I am after. Not for the tax office, but for Veronica, for Blokker, DKNY, Albert Heijn, BMW and Edah.

On television, they called her Becky. Her real name is Masja. She was also wearing a black wig. Weird, shiny curls – it was a cheap wig. She told about how she had weighed over 250 pounds, and now, after the operation and keeping her stomach wrapped, she never went over 150. Eating was hard, and sometimes it would come back up again, but she didn't regret it. It was her salvation. There was a whole row of the poor wretches sitting there, just like her. I don't remember what they looked like or what they said to Catherine Keijl. I do remember what I sat there screaming at her: you told Mother that you cry at night, that in the evenings you are sick, puking your guts out, you dream of eating a normal plate of food. That you only did it because Henk made you go back to work in the club, after all the illegal Polish and Czech whores were picked up. Because you didn't have the nerve to leave that sickhead. I know why you ate yourself into a blimp – out of sheer misery because you didn't want to keep working for that reprobate.

But okay, she didn't say all that. She wanted the money she'd get for her performance for Catherine. And the attention. There is not a lot of difference, whether you get paid for telling a television audience that you got sick from your addiction to food and that now you've had your stomach tied off or that you get paid for getting licked and screwed by middle managers from a trucking company in Zwolle. In both cases you do what you're expected to do. You adjust to your environment. You become a product, and money and attention briefly flow your way.

It was a small beginning. A grocery receipt. I found a mistaken receipt from the Albert Heijn in my bag. Somebody had bought a cake, on sale with the bonus card. They had the card in hand. The bill was tallied, including the discount. No sooner was it paid for, however, than he or she returned the cake and got the money back. And I saw a senile old man standing at the check-out with the cake. The cashier asked, Oh, Mr. Holten, is it somebody's birthday today? Yes, my wife's. Oh, says the girl, but I thought she was dead. And he is taken aback. He gives her back the cake and stands outside the store for a half hour in the drizzle, trying to get his head together, and then just walks on home.

For the company computers, the information from all those Albert Heijn slips is something like soil analysis is for an oil company. But the information has no face whatsoever, and selling is something you do to a face. When the telephone rang in the evening, the lad at the telemarketing centre called it my profile. Hundreds of questions about brand names, shops in the neighbourhood, my interests in sports, my political bent, my education. I wanted to tell him about Mr. Holten and his cake, but the fellow stuck to his list of questions and thought I was drunk. I became angry, which is of course not a good idea.

Consuming is an art in its own right. If you are good at it, people look up to you. Buying the right wristwatch in the right shop, the right corkscrew, or vase, or stocks, or telephone, is not only satisfying, but it makes you more attractive. That others find you attractive or that you can make them jealous and covetous is an indispensable attribute for borrowing money, having a nice job, sex opportunities, or getting people to pay attention to the things you want to say.

Homo Henk was in Amsterdam last week, to see an exhibition about advertising. It was called 'Advertisement Heroes', and he had brought home a couple of booklets and a folder. It all looked like jolly good nostalgic fun. Piggelmee the little Gnome, Joris Three-Pint, Loeki Lion, Put a Tiger in your Tank. But there was also a sentence that told what the reality of it all was like. Everybody is an advertising hero. Everybody plays a leading role, everyone is living his life like a commercial. There it stood, a little like parting respects to send you on your way.

Good, I think. So I will consume. But then I will really consume, so that there is nothing left over. The whole store, consumed, eaten up in one fell swoop, and count on it, I won't stuff myself so full of bon-bons that I have to hit the antacid pills. I will not consume with my wallet or my body, but with my fire. A great big bite, all the shelves bare, the whole store a flaming waste in the wake of a breathtakingly gorgeous ball if fire and a humming noise to go with it. My life will be a commercial for an imaginary company that – for free – surprises people with explosions and satisfies the public's need for release and relief, liberation and excitement. All for nothing at all. Not a penny. Actually, I am a commercial for a charitable institution and a hero in a commercial, a hero without the least trace of cynicism, with no hidden agenda. I do not believe in a Reaal insurance policy against damages or in a superior slender butter substitute, but in the universal, scorching purity of childlike pleasure in the BANG, BOOM, SWOOOSH.

I do not believe that I am a terrorist. For me it is not about changing the world. I do not want to blackmail a single figure of authority into changing his policies. And seducing the masses into thinking revolutionary thoughts is altogether a ridiculous objective. It is an error of judgement to think that other people have to think the way you do. They shouldn't know anything at all about what I think. That is much better. I just want a lot of exquisite explosions. It is just fine if they lead to nothing, absolutely nothing at all. Not to funerals, not panic-stricken governments or police, not to endless discussions in the papers and on news programmes. For my part, let the construction companies and the insurance companies profit from my actions, as long as people succeed in enjoying my explosions. There is nothing as NOW as an explosion. Nothing succeeds so fully in attracting all the attention, devouring and absorbing everything into a magical image. Fear and rapture. What I hope for is that after a while they will give up looking for me and resign themselves to the fact that now and then they will be treated to another BAM, BOOOSH, WHOOF!

Yesterday, I tried to write a letter to Masja. Not to send to her,but in case something should happen and I couldn't talk or write any more. A testament, say. It was late, there was no more Coke and I was drinking the Bacardi straight. I was watching a bunch of ludicrous, gaudily dressed idiots pressing a potato into an appliance so they could peel the thing with a crank. You ended up with a single long, stringy potato peel. It looked as though they were delighted by it.

What I nearly wrote – and god, how glad I am that I thought better of it – is this: that my explosions have no preconceived intentions and serve no purpose, that they are not a political act nor are they in any way whatsoever to my own advantage or provide me financial profit. For that reason, there was nothing else to it than to call them art. It looks a little like the delight they took in the potato peel. They apparently – certainly – want to sell that squeaky little cutter, so they act all excited about the irritating, mile-long peel. But why? It serves no purpose. It is a meaningless gesture. I, like many people, find explosions pure, powerful events, frightening and exhilarating, and maybe even more delightful because in the wink of an eye, they reduce everything to rubble. Why would I call it art? Does that make the disintegrating smithereens of the perfume boutique in Rijswijk a more beautiful sight to watch? Does the ball of fire become more intensely orange, the smoke blacker, the noise more thunderous?

Later, I lay in bed, surrendering, fairly paralytic, and I fantasized about an ideal world in which people offered me a meal and a bed, and hid me from the police. Friendly faces, people who like explosions, ordinary disbelievers like myself, who do not believe in the superiority of BMW, in the pureness of Grolsch beer or the high level of civilization achieved by the purchase of as complete an insurance package as possible. In my ideal world, I belong in the world, like the weather does, like a hailstorm. Even a hailstorm has its admirers, its friends. The politicians, the upholders of the law, the censors, the salesmen disapprove of my explosions, but they have learned to live with them. Lying here in my bed, I see myself travelling from city to city and everywhere I go, causing storefronts to spew fire, flames reaching high into the sky and big, billowing black clouds. Half asleep, I compare it all to the wandering minstrel who brings along his songs and his stories with him. Someone who travels on in exchange for a piece of bread, a sausage and a little beer. Childlike pleasure, inexhaustible, indestructible.

And so I fall asleep, forgetting my testament. As I sleep, I am not angry, not humiliated or left out. That is why I want to set my sleep-walking bombs and BANG, KABAAAAM! In an ideal world, I would succeed with nary a victim, making the joy of the celluloid blasts and those virtual onscreen explosions more real than real, a pure, fantasy image, out of nothing, about nothing, without consequences, without pain, sadness and loss. But everything would stop, just for that split second. The heat, the deafening volume, the shock wave, the concussion would all be real. For an instant there would be nothing more than the bloom of destruction, as glorious, perfect and empty as the clarity in the eye of a child singing aloud.

Good, I think. So I will consume. But then I will really consume, so that there is nothing left over.

DIRK VAN WEELDEN

OPPOSITIONS
DIRK VAN WEELDEN
Poetry
BARBARA DIJKHUIS
& Product
JANJAAP RIJPKEMA

Supermarket (1998) Like many designers, I am a collector. Packaging, tickets and associated paraphernalia adorn my walls. I will often use these at a later date in a design, or they will trigger another idea. I reuse, as it were, elements in the visual culture around me and put them into another context, whereby they change their meaning. For me, it is a good way to communicate with people. There is a keen sense of recognition and you increase the level of attention you attribute to everyday matters. The people who use them, of course, are also part of our visual culture. I find it fascinating to see how people behave in a (designed) environment.

These interests converge in the phenomenon of the supermarket. First, there is the external appearance of the supermarket. All those products, decked out all along the shelves in their Sunday best, screaming for you to notice them. The sense of wealth and privilege that you feel because of the sheer numbers of them. On the other hand, there is the game between the consumer, the products and the retailer. How do they respond to one another and what is this 'fight' that they are engaged in, in this theatre of the supermarket?

I took the metaphor of the theatre as a cornerstone for my graduate project. The seduction and the drama(tics) that you experience when you walk through a supermarket, as opposed to the changing décor of the shelves, can be experienced as a performance. In the exhibition, I show a compilation of my visual study and the resulting final project. I have dealt with the two on as equal terms as possible, because the presentation was an exhibition that cannot be repeated, and because the visual study was a substantial part of the final project.

On the other hand, I have also illustrated the theatrical aspect of the supermarket in more subtle fashion, in the form of a book. As its starting point, I used the cashier's receipt. The receipt is the two-dimensional translation of the grocery cart, and of a personal choice from a broad selection of products on offer. On that receipt, not only the products purchased make up part of the 'scenario', but also the peripheral information, such as the date, time and the name of the supermarket. All of this information makes the grocery receipt an intimate document. I have selected fifty of these human 'portraits', and brought them onto the stage of a poetry collection.

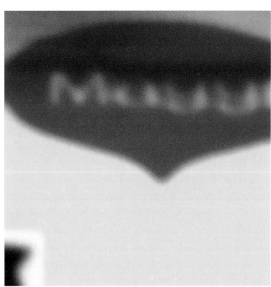

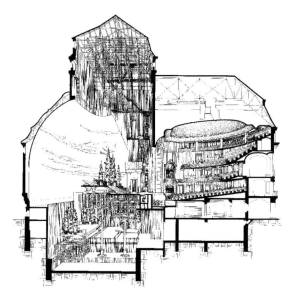

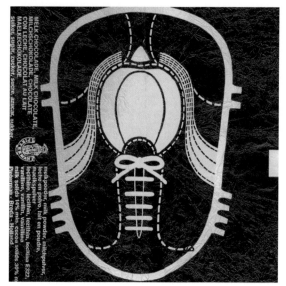

previous pages:
Images from the visual essay on the supermarket

right:
As part of the supermarket study, I conducted a test to see how easily colour and form remain recognizable in images of a brand or group of products

```
          A & P
    Ginnekenweg 46
     4818 JG  Breda
   Tel.nr.: 076-5147908
   ------------------------


TAART                 8,99
** CORRECTIE **
TAART                 8,99-
                    --------
Subtotaal             0,00
Terug                 0,00

Bedrag zonder BTW     0,00


Kassa 006/0012  Bon 0247 PC02 P
Datum 31-03-98  Tijd 14:01 #

    Openingstijden A&P
  Ma,Di+Wo: 08.00-20.00
       Do: 08.00-21.00
       Vr: 08.00-20.00
       Za: 08.00-18.00




          A & P
    Ginnekenweg 46
     4818 JG  Breda
   Tel.nr.: 076-5147908
   ------------------------


WEGW.BEKER            2,09
POEDERSUIKER          0,89
ROERSTAAF             2,09
SLAGROOM PK           1,99
SLAGROOM PK           1,99
ELSTAR                3,18
                    --------
Subtotaal            12,23
Afgerond             12,25
        KONTANT      12,25
Terug                 0,00

6,00% uit     8,05    0,46
17,50% uit    4,18    0,62
Bedrag zonder BTW    11,15


Kassa 002/0004  Bon 0005 PC01 P
Datum 01-04-98  Tijd 08:16 #   6

    Openingstijden A&P
  Ma,Di+Wo: 08.00-20.00
       Do: 08.00-21.00
       Vr: 08.00-20.00
       Za: 08.00-18.00
```

```
ALBERT HEIJN BREDA
VALKENIERSPLEIN 2
TEL: 076-5654380

                          f

AM KAARTNR.: 0121865452
COCA-COLA             2,39
+STATIE FLES          1,00
SPRUITEN              0,99
DRAAGTAS KLN          0,35
JEU DE BOULE          3,99
NAVELS 3 KG           7,50
COOLBEST             2,49
HALFV MELK            1,53
GOUDS L BEL           7,67
AQUAFR F&C            4,60
KIT KAT MINI          3,79
RB SPECULAAS          3,99
OLVARIT 436           2,09
OLVARIT 440           2,09
OLV FRUIT             2,29
OLV FRUIT             2,29
OLVARIT 415           2,09
OLVARIT 405           2,09
OLVARIT 425           2,29
OLVARIT 425           2,29
OLVARIT 403           2,09
OLVARIT 425           2,29
OLVARIT 407           2,09
OLVARIT 426           2,29
OLV FRUIT             2,29
OLVARIT 404           2,09
OLVARIT 403           2,09
OLVARIT 404           2,09
OLVARIT 426           2,29
OLVARIT 405           2,09
OLVARIT 426           2,29

SUBTOTAAL            81,80

AKTIE BABYV.-10%
      KORTING
      10% x  f41,51  -4,15

SUBTOTAAL            77,65
TOTAAL               77,65

EMBALLAGEBON          2,00
TE BETALEN           75,65

CONTANT             101,00
TERUG                25,35

1045  5    202        8
17:54         13-11-1997

HARTELIJK BEDANKT VOOR UW
BEZOEK EN GRAAG TOT ZIENS.
```

```
          A & P
    Ginnekenweg 46
     4818 JG  Breda
   Tel.nr.: 076-5147908
   ------------------------


OMWISSELEN

*******************************

Kassa 006/0008  Bon 0278 PC02 P
Datum 01-04-98  Tijd 16:54 #

    Openingstijden A&P
  Ma,Di+Wo: 08.00-20.00
       Do: 08.00-21.00
       Vr: 08.00-20.00
       Za: 08.00-18.00




          A & P
    Ginnekenweg 46
     4818 JG  Breda
   Tel.nr.: 076-5147908
   ------------------------


OPPERBIER             9,36
STATIEGELD            8,60
OPPERBIER             9,36
STATIEGELD            8,60
OPPERBIER             9,36
STATIEGELD            8,60
                    --------
Subtotaal            53,88
FLESSENBON           24,15-
                    --------
Subtotaal            29,73
Afgerond             29,75
        KONTANT      30,00
Terug                 0,25

17,50% uit    28,08   4,18
Bedrag zonder BTW    25,55


Kassa 002/0004  Bon 0116 PC01 P
Datum 01-04-98  Tijd 11:55 #   3

    Openingstijden A&P
  Ma,Di+Wo: 08.00-20.00
       Do: 08.00-21.00
       Vr: 08.00-20.00
       Za: 08.00-18.00
```

DIRK VAN DEN BROEK
HEEFT HET LAAGSTE
PRIJSPEIL VAN NEDERLAND !

BOS EN LOMMERPLEIN 1
020-4880092

WOE 08-04-98   %0006

115vk   E.VEREIJKEN

BOTERHAMZAKJES   0,89
DIEPVRIESZAKJE   0,79
SUBTOT   1,68

TOTAAL   **1,68**

ONTVANGEN   10,00
TERUGGAVE   8,30

2514%   2 art   11:02hr

BASISMARKT
VALKENIERSPLEIN 8
BREDA
**BEDANKT
EN TOT ZIENS**

WOE 10-12-97   %0002

111vk

SCHARRELEIEREN   2,49
PINDAKAAS   0,89
APPELMOES   0,79
SUB-TOTAAL   4,17

TOTAAL   4,17

ONTVANGEN   5,15
TERUGGAVE   1,00

0379%   3 art   17:02hr

DIRK VAN DEN BROEK
HEEFT HET LAAGSTE
PRIJSPEIL VAN NEDERLAND !

BOS EN LOMMERPLEIN 1
020-4880092

WOE 08-04-98   %0006

140vk   G.HILVERTS

SALADE   1,89
3-ES UP   0,35
3-ES UP   0,35
3 ES COLA   0,35
3 ES COLA   0,35
FANTA BLIK   0,75
FANTA BLIK   0,75
SHANDY BLIK   0,89
SHANDY BLIK   0,89
SINASDRINK 6/1   1,75
APPELSAP 6/1   1,99
CHOCOLADEMELK   1,89
VOLLE MELK   1,33
WHISKAS   1,69
TIJGERNOOTJES   2,49
SILAN   2,98
PAL   1,69
PAL   1,69
CHOCO PINDA'S   2,98
LOLLIES   1,89
LOLLIES   1,89
LOLLIES   1,89
WHISKAS   1,69
DORITOS   1,99
ZOUTE STICKS   0,79
TOILETPAPIER   3,29
ZOUTJES   1,89
BUGLES   1,89
SUPERCHIPS   1,99
KAASKNABBELS   0,99
HEEL WIT   0,95
MINI FRITES   1,19
SALAMI   2,89
DRAAGTAS   0,25
SUBTOT   52,52

TOTAAL   **52,52**

ONTVANGEN   55,00
TERUGGAVE   2,50

2676%   34 art   13:33hr

A&P SIG.HUL*   1,99
** **CORRECTIE** **
A&P SIG.HUL*   1,99-
** **HERSTEL** **
MAGR.BOSVR.   3,19-
VANILLE VLA*   1,85

Subtotaal   3,02
Afgerond   3,00
          KONTANT   3,00
Terug   0,00

6,00% uit   3,02   0,17
Bedrag zonder BTW   2,85

Kassa 001/0006 Bon 0043 PC01 P
Datum 01-04-98 Tijd 17:43 #   2

Openingstijden A&P
Ma,Di+Wo: 08.00-20.00
      Do: 08.00-21.00
      Vr: 08.00-20.00
      Za: 08.00-18.00

Gulden Winckelplantsoen 13
020-6870190
SPAAR VOOR GESCHENKEN
UIT DE KADO WINKEL

AANT	OMSCHRIJVING	PRIJS	BEDRAG
1	CANDYMAN VRUCHTENPAAL	1.69	1.69
1	SUBTOTAAL		1.69

TOTAAL   **1.70**
KONTANT   **10.00**
WISSELGELD   **8.30**

Bon-0387 Kassa-02 Kassiere-002 - 08.04.98 - 14.24.26

OPPOSITIONS

DIRK VAN WEELDEN
Poetry
BARBARA DIJKHUIS
& Product
JANJAAP RIJPKEMA

Explosion World® (1999)

Explosion World® brings together a number of ideas and interests. In the first place, I am interested in the narrative aspects of architecture, in how a building tells a story. A façade suggests something hidden behind that exterior, whereas what is actually behind it is sometimes something quite different, or maybe there is nothing at all. I am also interested in prefabricated architecture. Modular building makes it possible, at little expense and in rapid tempo, to build in large volume. For many builidings , an architect is hardly required. Prefab buildings currently in existence do have the tendency to look very much alike. For that reason, I ask myself whether the manner in which a building tells its story can in fact be prefabricated. The means that might be employed to achieve this could include the module form, the finishing or detail, the 'skin' and lettering.

These two interests come together in the theme park. Here, with its attractions, all the visual and commercial disciplines combine to achieve a certain effect. In the theme park, utopia is made plastic – and plastified. Techniques are employed to disguise these same techniques. In this paradise, history is applied in the form of tableaux that disfigure that same history, forming it into an attractive archetype. It is not about a past we collectively share, but about a fantasy scenario with a happy ending.

Finally, the increasing media attention to violence in our society has not escaped my attention. On the one hand, violence and excessive strength are exalted. On the other hand, they become demonic as soon as they appear in our personal living environment. Physical violence leads to social unrest, but is in my opinion not the only cause. Non-physical, structural violence lies at its roots.

The Explosion World® amusement park has violence as its basic theme. In Explosion World®, the visitor can at last experience a bombing from close by, live through a fire in a high-rise apartment building, take a tour of Dante's Hell and even blow themselves up. Explosion World® is a theme park that plays on our yearning for the sensation of danger and violence. Violence as amusement.

Despite the appearance of danger, evoked by every conceivable means, the safety regulations in the park are extremely strict, not only because there is the threat of danger, but also because it

I have already been waiting for the blast for so long. The real one, the one that only appears when the explosion is so huge and so beautiful that you forget what went into the air.

DIRK VAN WEELDEN

promotes efficient business and prevents legal claims. After Disney World, Explosion World® is the safest place on earth.

I have developed the project in two parts. The first is made up of promotional material targeting the fictional visitors to the park. The second part shows how maintenance and service personnel (from temporary job agencies) have to respond in certain situations. I have tried to make it possible to imagine such a park, down to the details.

Redecorate structures from the past.

Explosion World™

War was what people did before there was Explosion World™.

Explosion World™

We hired the UNA bomber; as our interior decorator.

Explosion World™

Benefit from instability.

Explosion World™

Shifts in morality are opportunities.

Explosion World™

More orange on our streets.

Explosion World™

Fun is well spent boredom.

Explosion World™

Think in Worlds.

Explosion World™

Boredom is the flywheel of capitalism.

Explosion™ World

The past deserves to be made entertaining.

Explosion™ World

Suck the youth out of the young.

Explosion™ World

Improve natural disasters.

Explosion™ World

Be a warlord in suburbia.

Explosion™ World

The whole world is imitating US.

Explosion™ World

Racism is too expensive.

Explosion™ World

Philosophy #1

Explosion World Corporate philosophy. Part 1-17, from a series of 200. Flyers, books and posters.

Philosopy #2
PRESENTATIONS AND TRAINING

Explosi**o**n™ w**o**rld

for more information or free collectible cards
mail: explosionworld@freemail.nl

cooperating contradictions®

sheet #1 of 5   ©the xplosion company®   Explosi**o**n™ w**o**rld

mass	⟨⟩	individual
experience	⟨⟩	artificiality
pleasure	⟨⟩	pain
nostalgia	⟨⟩	fear
Hollywood	⟨⟩	Oklahoma
Bruce Willis	⟨⟩	Una bomber
Cool (kewl)	⟨⟩	Bad (Bêêêd)
luxury	⟨⟩	destruction
phantasy	⟨⟩	reality
phantarality		fearalisy
outdoor-ism	⟨⟩	mall-ism
consumers	⟨⟩	participants
Gulf war	⟨⟩	Private Ryan

above: Investors meeting, April 1997, Okura Hotel Amsterdam
left: *'Coöperating Contradictions™' Moodboard from a Management training session.*
right: *Page from a physical test manual for recruited employees.*

A Typical Qualifying Physical Fitness Test for an Explosion World employee

Instructions for Candidates

These subtests are electronically timed by your stepping on the Start Mat and the Finish Mat.

STAIR CLIMB/RESTRAIN: (One Trial)
(Maximum Time Allowed: Two Minutes)

In this subtest, you will be expected to run up 3 flights of stairs, down 1 flight, push and pull a box 5 times, and run 5 feet to the finish line.

* On the signal GO, step on the Start Mat, run up the stairs on your right, and continue up to the landing on the third floor.
* Both feet must be placed on the landing.
* Run quickly down one flight of stairs and into the lobby.

THE POLICE OFFICER SCREENING PROCESS

* Grab the box and pull it towards you until the front of the box reaches the tape on the floor.
* Now push it back to its starting position.
* Repeat 4 more times as the examiner announces the count.
* After the last trip, turn RIGHT and step on the Finish Mat.

DUMMY DRAG: (Two Trials)
(Maximum Time Allowed: One Minute)

In this subtest, you will be expected to drag a dummy 30 feet.

* Step on the Start Mat.
* Grab the dummy under the shoulders.
* Holding the dummy in this position, move backwards around the traffic cone set 15 feet away and return.
* Place the dummy EXACTLY as you found it in the starting position.
* Step on the Finish Mat.

WALL CLIMB/OBSTACLE RUN: (Two Trials)
(Maximum Time Allowed: One Minute)

In this subtest, you will be expected to go over the 5-foot wall and continue through the obstacle run.

* Step on the Start Mat.
* Run to the wall and go over. You are NOT allowed to use the support bars.
* Follow the tape on the floor around the cones.
* If you miss a cone or go around it the wrong way, you must go back and go around the cone CORRECTLY.
* If you knock a cone over, you must STOP and set it up before you continue.
* Step on the Finish Mat.

Attractions

A SELECTION OF EXPLOSION WORLD'S BIGGEST AND MOST POPULAR FEATURES

for more information or free collectible cards
mail: explosionworld@freemail.nl

The Arcade

Explosion world

Dante's Inferno

Explosion world

above: *The Arcade®. A shrine for shoot'm up games characters.*
left: *Dante's Inferno®. A breath-taking tour through Dante's Hell*

Attractions

A SELECTION OF EXPLOSION WORLD'S BIGGEST AND MOST POPULAR FEATURES

Explosion ™ world

for more information or free collectible cards
mail: explosionworld@freemail.nl

PortaCabin® City

Napalm Park

above: *Portacabin City®.*
The heart of Explosion City, in the heart of Explosion World. Enjoy luxurious consumption with the thrill of violent surprises.
left: *Napalm Park®.*
Cherish throbbing adrenaline when Napalm-bombed by F15 Hornets.
above right: *Bikini Beach Plaza®.*
Get an experimantal tan, while our scientists heat up this paradise.
right: *Highway of hell®.*
The most spectacular chases and Car crashes observed from four luxuruous vista points.

Merchandise

A SELECTION OF EXPLOSION WORLD'S MERCHANDISE

for more information or free collectible cards
mail: explosionworld@freemail.nl

Clockwise:
- *I Love Explosion World™- Logo,
  applied on stickers, T-shirts,
  Lunchboxes etc.*
- *Shared Action Marketing with
  big corporations.*
- *Free computer game, distributed
  through schools and playgrounds*
- *Explosion World™ Trooper Uniform.
  Includes subscription to a magazine
  and membership in Explosive-
  Troopers®.*
- *Explosion World™ Brochure*

Logistics
SAMPLES OF
LOGISTIC SYSTEMS

for more information or free collectible cards
mail: explosionworld@freemail.nl

lower-management
business call

middle-management
business call

higher-management
business call

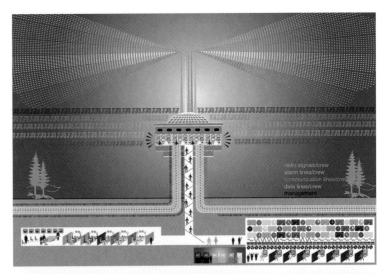

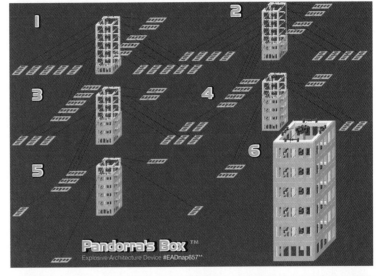

above: *Page from a Management behaviour instruction manual.*
above right: *Explosion World™ controltower and central control basement.*
right middle: *Rendering of Pandorra's Box' contruction.*
below right: *Evacuation Procedure for technical employees.*

Logistics

above: *Parking and storage lots for the 'Highway of Hell' attraction*
below: *Cross-section of CityBlow™-Main Street.*

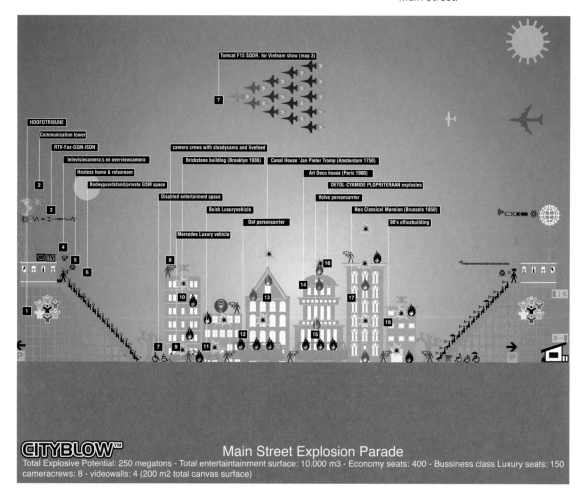

Tomcat F15 SQDR. for Vietnam show (map 3)

HOOFDTRIBUNE

Communication tower

RTV-Fax-GSM-ISDN

televisiecamera;s en overviewcamera

camera crews with steadycams and livefeed

Hostess home & relaxroom

Brickstone building (Brooklyn 1930)

Canal House 'Jan Pieter Tromp (Amsterdam 1750)

Bodeyguardstand/private GSM space

Art Deco house (Paris 1900)

DETOL-CYAMIDE PLOPRITERAAN explosies

Disabled entertainment space

Volvo personcarrier

Buick Luxuryvehicle

Neo Classical Mansion (Brussels 1850)

Daf personcarrier

90's officebuilding

Mercedes Luxury vehicle

CITYBLOW™ Main Street Explosion Parade
Total Explosive Potential: 250 megatons - Total entertaintainment surface: 10.000 m3 - Economy seats: 400 - Bussiness class Luxury seats: 150 cameracrews: 8 - videowalls: 4 (200 m2 total canvas surface)

Largitecture

SAMPLES OF PRE-FAB
CONSTRUCTIONS FROM CON-
STRUCTION EMPLOYEES MANUAL

for more information or free collectible cards
mail: explosionworld@freemail.nl

Façade Unit 'Vinex Pride'

Stackable Portacabin Unit 'Sobriety'

Public Space Unit - 'Darth Vader'™

Portable Chemical Lab 'Columbaine'

Park Unit ' Flamingo'

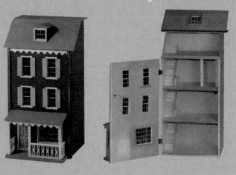

OPPOSITIONS

MARTIN REINTS
Story
PAULINE HOOGWEG
& Collectivity
GERARD FOX

The Power of the Cliché The suburban neighbourhoods: they typify what is now the last century. They came about as healthy transitional districts for the overcrowded city, whose 17th-century centre would now be called the inner city. The contrast between city and countryside became blurred. In the city itself, the countryside pushed its way back in, in the form of green patches and parks. In the outlying neighbourhoods, the city imposed itself with roads and public transport.

In the second half of the last century, an important percentage of employment facilities moved from the cities to outlying industrial parks. In between the more expensive offices that remained in the city centre, a new social life emerged in the evenings, nights and weekends. Taking walks in the neighbourhood you lived in or in the landscape along the edges of town fell out of fashion and disappeared. A leftover of that seems to have survived in the form of grocery shopping. The suburban neighbourhood is somewhat urban in character because it is inhabited by city people, but it is also like a village, lacking urban facilities. What can you say about it? What else, except that – as they say – there's nothing happening?

In 1935, Martinus Nijhoff held what has since become his famous lecture for the Volksuniversiteit in Enschede, about 'making verses in times of crisis' and how his book, Awater came about. There is a passage from his lecture about the suburban neighbourhoods of his day, of which he said, 'If I walk through the new neighbourhood, built on lease and speculation, I walk through a house of cards, where people eat badly, heat their homes badly and only care for one another out of fear of loneliness. The compact city centre, which has already been there for centuries, will remain standing for centuries longer than those hopeless little 'garden' cities, with their front gardens and coloured floor lamps. In what way must poetry make this virtually loose sand habitable again?'

The hopeless garden cities against the age-old little city centre. Nijhoff put his finger on a far-reaching development. His view of how crowds form was characteristic of his day: 'I began to see that people did not live in the unreal little houses in the outlying neighbourhoods, houses that stood like tents in the landscape. Where people lived was in the offices, the factories, the hospitals, the cafes, the train stations, in all the places where masses of people came together.'

It is a familiar image: the crowds moving through the bustling inner city. It was sketched in so many impressive books and films from the first half of the 20th century, that it became the ultimate image of the modern age. In the meantime, just out of sight of one another, one new neighbourhood after the other was cropping up, but that fact was not included – it was too unreal. That is to say, the post-war rise of the suburbs was extensively documented, because it was the metaphor for the reconstruction. The fallow earth of the building sites, the cement mixers, the pile-driving, the bricklaying, new residents moving into the umpteen-hundred-thousandth home, the design of the kitchen – all of this was depicted. But life in the suburb, this was hardly a subject of discussion. If it was spoken of at all, it was in caricature fashion.

It would appear that in our day, everyday life has been rediscovered. In Rotterdam in 1993, a large-scale festival was devoted to the architecture of the Alexander Polder. Photographers such as Nick Waplington and Jean Louis Schoelkopf made documentaries centred on the residents of the neighbourhood. Waplington took panoramic pictures of home interiors, with the intention of making not only their similarities evident, but also their differences. Schoelkopf said he was fascinated by the way people who lived in a given type of uniform housing were able to express themselves in the interior. This kind of documentary photography cut into the caricatured image of these neighbourhoods, because the focus was on neither the mass nor the monotonous, but on the individual who in fact distinguishes himself, always and everywhere.

One also comes across similarly serious attention to life in these neighbourhoods in painting and in literature. In August of 1995, an issue of De Gids (the Guide) was entirely devoted to suburban neighbourhoods, and included contributions by Rem Koolhaas, Dirk van Weelden and Wouter Klootwijk. The problem facing anyone who wants to say something about these neighbourhoods is that there is a caricature in the way, a stereotype. The cliché is insurmountable. You first have to manage to distract people's attention from the cliché, because only then can your public apprehend what you are trying to show.

Gerard Fox's visual stories deal adroitly with the cliché. For him, the neighbourhood is the self-evident environment for what seem like events, but if you want to put together a cohesive story about it, you confront a shortage of facts. The fantasy that is consequently set in motion makes the viewer part of the story. The collages of a children's party in a back garden, of an interior with a television in it, of the traffic in the street – they are called visual stories, but they barely tell a story at all. Because of the familiar details, the image too is familiar. But because it is not clear exactly what is going on, your curiosity is aroused and your gaze begins working through the details of the collage. From that moment on, you have shaken loose the caricature of these neighbourhoods that has existed for so long, and you begin to have an eye for the reality that is taking place. Gerard Fox's way of approaching the clichés from which his tale is composed is festive and satisfying. He has developed a means of saying something about the cliché by using the cliché.

A poem by Pauline Hoogweg is comprised of a series of short, understandable sentences, a blank line and a concluding familiar saying such as, 'The early bird catches the worm,' or a clichéd expression: 'You can bet your boots on that'. The texts consequently take on the structure of emblemata, the texts used as captions on 17th-century engravings. The engravings illustrated the expressions, the texts gave the explanation and the saying or expression itself was the superscript or subtitle.

Approximately the same thing happens in Pauline Hoogweg's use of language as in Gerard Fox's images. Your attention is drawn to the clichéd captions beneath the text. If the cliché were above the texts, you would probably have quickly decided that there was no need to read further. This presentation, however, arouses your curiosity, and now you have a series of sentences to read that are not difficult to understand, but that together, tell so incomplete a story that they cannot serve as a self-evident reinforcement of the cliché. A good example: He won't tell anyone/How he learned to dance.//All's well that ends well.

It is a very big cliché: All's well that ends well. Its history is difficult to trace. The expression is in any case far older than the phenomenon of the suburban community, and the original significance of such a worn-out phrase hardly even registers any more. But the idea of someone who will not tell anyone how he learned to dance is so mysterious that it captures your attention. As a reader, you want to put together a logical story about it, but again, you do not have enough facts. Why won't this protagonist tell his silly story about learning to dance? By way of the cliché, your mind comes to rest on what seems to me to be the actual subject of the text: what is there about dancing that is interesting, how do you learn to dance, how private can something that you do in public be? And what is good about an ending? And if the ending is good, does that make everything good? What does that entail? Pauline Hoogweg combines these emblematic texts with photographs of unprepossessing scenes that attract your attention because of the way they are cropped and removed from the setting. This combination adds yet a little more tension to the generalities in her texts.

Gerard Fox and Pauline Hoogweg have both succeeded in using the cliché in such a way that the focus of the cliché is redirected, leaning to something as ordinary as a suburb or someone who learned to dance. They do not do so with the duplicitous pleasure of someone who stands aloof from the commonplace, but with the involvement of someone openly trying to see. One designer focuses on the outer urban neighbourhood, the other on generally accepted sayings or expressions. Because they have dealt with the cliché in a non-clichéd manner, they both give their subject back its original power. The strength of their work is the strength of the cliché.

OPPOSITIONS
MARTIN REINTS
Story
PAULINE HOOGWEG
& Collectivity
GERARD FOX

And How a Cow Catches a Hare Fresh Morale (1997). I am a reporter. On the sidelines, off the field, I camouflage myself. I listen to the things that happen and the memories they leave behind. I rearrange them as my own memory inspires me to do. The result is a story, whether or not it really happened, but in any case convincing, in the sense that you want to believe in it and allot some space to the things it contains. The story offers a temporary order, something to grasp onto.

Fresh Morale: A Word on Proverbs Interested in the cliché because of the lack of nuance in the way it expresses something, it was taken for granted that I would run into its kindred phenomenon, the proverb. The proverb proved even more adept at relating self-satisfied truths. The manner of the telling has so much magical clarity that you are quickly inclined to believe in it. I became curious how true the truth was that is spoken by the proverb, and whether we were here concerned with a genuine philosopher or just a clever charlatan. The idea of putting it to the test began to evolve.

A Word on Proverbs in Regards to My Project I wanted to test both the flexibility and the degree of truth in the proverb, and to do so by means of short tales or films in which events from real life (this as a partial concession to the proverb – everyday life is after all its common arena) are told and subsequently coupled to a proverb. The story or film relates an anecdote, a small drama, and the proverb follows as a postscript. The resulting relationship can evolve in all sorts of ways, as long as an exchange takes place between the two. This interchange can comprise the story cancelling out the moral of the proverb, or the other way around, with the proverb putting an entirely new light on the story. This is made metaphoric – cutting, syrupy, dry or brought into perspective – by way of humour, emotion, disorientation, observation or surprise.

The story, as it were, pushes the proverb to the edge of the precipice, and it goes into a free fall. It remains to be seen if it finds its footing.

All's well that ends well? What can be good about an end? And if the end is good, is everything good?

MARTIN REINTS

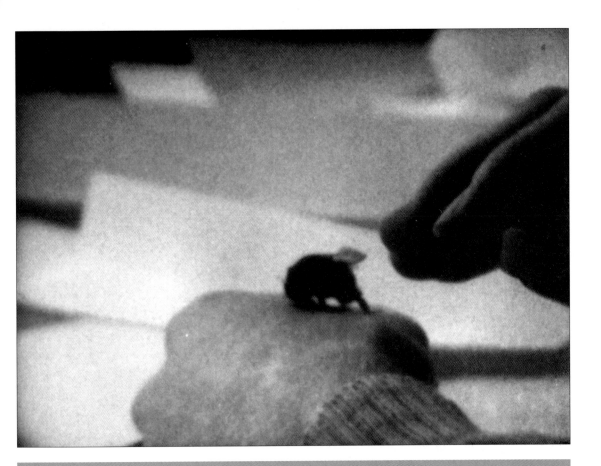

De kip legt een haan
de haan legt een ei
het ei komt uit
de uitkomst loopt weg

Hoe een koe een haas vangt

The hen lays a rooster
rooster lays an egg
out comes the chic
the hatchling's away

You never know your luck

Hij zegt niets maar
vraagt wat er te koop is
hij laat zijn gezicht zien
verbergt zijn handen in zijn zakken
hij vraagt hoeveel het kost
er is niets te koop
men kan het wel proberen
maar het is heel moeilijk

De kat uit de boom kijken

He says nothing more
asks what's for sale
he shows his face
hides his hands in his pockets
asks how much it costs
there is nothing for sale
it is very hard
try what you will

See which way the wind blows

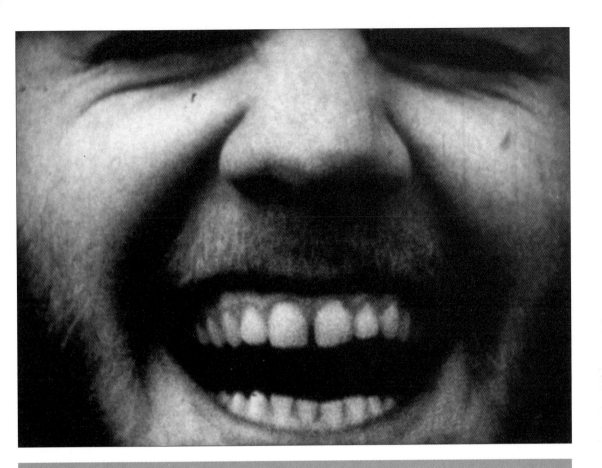

Het ruikt naar winter	It smells of winter
het ruikt naar lente	it smells of spring
het is de geur van het weer	it is the scent of the weather
hij trekt zijn laarzen aan	he puts on his boots
hij vergeet zijn handschoenen niet	doesn't forget his gloves
hij bedenkt zijn hoed	thinks of his had
hij zet hem op	puts it on his head
hij pakt zijn sjaal	picks up his scarf
en kijkt in de spiegel	and looks in the mirror
de lok valt voor zijn gezicht	the hair falls in his eyes
hij veegt hem weg	he sweeps it back
de vrouw staat achter hem	the woman is behind him
hij pakt zijn geweer	he takes his gun
en draait zich om	and turns around
zijn hoed zakt scheef	his hat sags
zijn mond valt open	his mouth drops open
Al is de leugen nog zo snel,	However swift the lie,
de waarheid achterhaalt haar wel	the truth will out

De vogel in de lucht zingt zijn lied	The bird in the air sings his song
de lucht ziet grauw	the air is grey
de zon schijnt niet	the sun does not shine
het licht is grijs	the light is grey
de straten zijn grijs	the streets are grey
de huizen en mensen	the houses and the people
het grijs is geel en licht	the grey is yellow and light
de vogel zingt, de koe loeit	the bird sings, the cow bellows
de koeien loeien, de vogels zingen	the cows bellow, the birds sing
de hond blaft, het paard hinnikt	the dog barks, the horse whinnies
de dag breekt aan, de zon schijnt	the day breaks, the sun shines
iedereen gaat er snel vandoor	everybody leaves in a hurry

De morgenstond brengt
goud in de mond

The early bird catches the worm

Hij ligt in de tent	He lies in the tent
de wind waarschuwt	the wind a warning
hij hoort de wind	he hears the wind
de haringen zitten los	the herrings are loose
hij trekt het doek	he pulls the cloth
nog strakker om zich heen	more tightly around him

Die waagt, die wint   **Nothing ventured, nothing gained**

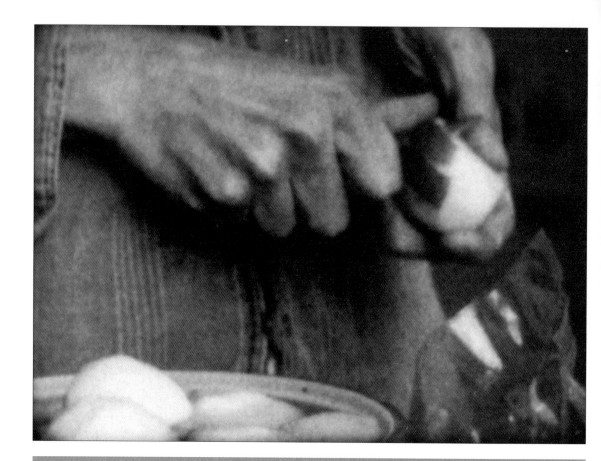

De vissenkom staat op de plank	The fishbowl is on the shelf
de papieren worden nat	the papers are wet
de vissen zwemmen	it's raining marbles
het regent knikkers	they fall and clatter
ze vallen en klinken	the door opens
de deur gaat open	the fish swim around it
de vissen zwemmen er omheen	the bowls runs empty
de kom loopt leeg	

Wie niet sterk is, moet slim zijn   If the lion's skin cannot, the fox's shall

De vogels schrikken op	The birds take flight
hij komt er aan	as he comes
hij heeft het voer	he has the food
de vogels hangen aan het gaas	in the wire they hang
ze zijn fladderig	flittering
nerveus en geel met rood	nervous and yellow and red
ze hebben geen honger	not hungry
ze weten wat ze krijgen	they know what they are getting
ze krijgen meelwormen	they've had enough
ze hebben er genoeg van	mealworms

De één zijn brood
is de ander zijn dood

Breath to one is death to another

Hij blijft liggen in bed	He stays there lying in bed
hij droomt van een prinses	he dreams of a princess
zij rijdt auto	driving a car
ze razen over de snelweg	they race along the highway
hij grist het stuur uit haar handen	he grabs the wheel from her hands
nog net op tijd staan ze stil	they stop just in time
hij stapt uit	he gets out
en zwaait naar haar	and waves to her

Zo gewonnen, zo geronnen   Easy come, easy go

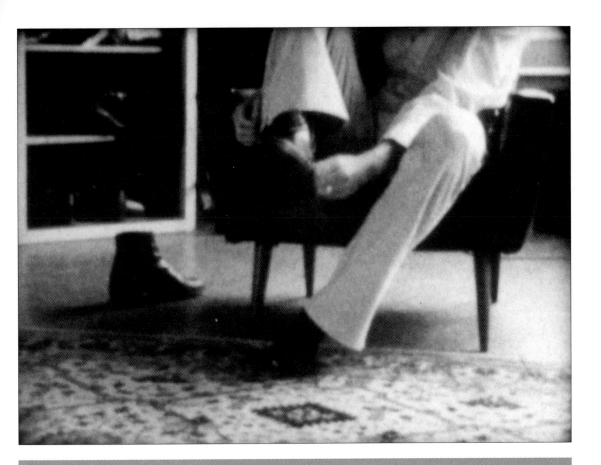

De stoel aan de tafel schuift aan	The chair at the table slides in
de stoel aan de tafel schuift weg	the chair at the table slides out
de stoel aan de tafel valt om	the chair at the table falls over
trekt het tafelkleed mee	it pulls the tablecloth
trekt de kopjes mee	pulls the cups
de koekjes mee	pulls the cookies
de suiker mee	the sugar
de lepeltjes mee	the spoons
de melk mee	the milk
de sigaretten en asbak	the cigarettes and ashtray
en kranten mee	and newspapers
de schoteltjes blijven staan	the saucers stay where they are
De wonderen zijn de wereld niet uit	Will wonders never cease

Hij weet een plek	He knows a place
die plek	that place
daar wil hij heen	that's where he wants to go
hij gaat	he goes
de rivier maakt geluid	the river makes noises
het ruist en spettert	it rushes and spatters
beneden hem is er geroep	below him a call
hij hoort stemmen	he hears voices
hij versnelt zijn pas	he quickens his pace
daar struikelt hij	there he struggles
ze roepen hem	they call him
hij zegt niets	he says nothing
hij verraadt niemand	he betrays no one
hij glimlacht in het gras	he smiles in the grass

Een goed begin is het halve werk   A good beginning is half the work

Hoe hij heeft leren dansen
vertelt hij aan niemand

He won't tell anyone
How he learned to dance

Eind goed, al goed

All's well that ends well

OPPOSITIONS
MARTIN REINTS
Story
PAULINE HOOGWEG
& Collectivity
GERARD FOX

Suburbia (1999) We make our buildings, then our buildings make us: The term Suburb refers to a residential area usually found on the periphery of a city. It is the meeting point between urban and rural. The literal meaning of the word Suburb is geographic. It refers to the physical structuring of the archetypal suburb. However, the term Suburbia refers to the social and cultural sphere existing within this structure. The Suburb is the hardware, Suburbia is the software. It is this software that is of most relevance to my project.

Dublin Suburbs Dublin city contains some of the fastest expanding suburban sprawl in Europe. On the western outskirts of the city are situated large clusters of large suburban areas. Little of this housing is based on European public high-rise housing schemes, but is more in tune with the American model of private low-rise homes. It is this model that Dubliners have developed in the last thirty years. 'Houses, houses everywhere and not much else'. Every suburban cluster is linked to the city-centre via motorway. Dublin seems to be a city spreading out and onwards never looking back.

There are problems,   The private housing developers who are responsible for much of this suburban form will argue that they are completely justified in continuing to build this same sameness claiming that people will not buy what they don't want. (They also face little resistance in the form of planning regulations or civil law). Therefore they continue to build what is cheapest and what has been proven to sell. Considering that tax incentives and government housing grants for home buyers heavily favour the purchasing of newly erected housing, the first-time house buyer can often be faced with no real housing alternative except to buy one of these units. This situation exists simply to encourage the city's construction industry, an industry which is believed to play an integral role in the progress of the state economy. Unfortunately this all continues to happen with little or no regard for the consequences upon the city, thus fanning the flames of the city's suburban sprawl.

In these areas of the city, implementation of 'infrastructure' is somewhat inconsistent. These suburban clusters have begun to spawn their own Americana style 'Mega-Shopping Malls' (shops, cinema, Bowling alley...etc.) finally providing local service and employment needs. Through the implementation of government tax incentives, international manufacturing companies have also

The problem facing anyone who wants to say something about these neighbourhoods is that there is a caricature in the way, a stereotype.

MARTIN REINTS

recently begun to established factories in local industrial estates thus providing more local employment. Unfortunately these developments have all come to pass twenty-five years after some of these areas were originally established.

The suburban housing of Dublin has changed little in form or format over the past thirty years. The only change; each individual housing unit continues to get smaller.

Influence   The influence of the post-war suburb on contemporary western lifestyles is unquestionable. It has contributed to the fashioning of nearly every aspcct of today's generic 'home'. The domesticated identity of Suburbia has been moulded by its representation through popular culture and the general mass media. It both feeds from and is fed by its own image. The symptoms of this suburban identity contribute to an already accelerating process of global cultural homogenisation. From the commercial media through to children's education, the Suburban tract house 'home' is portrayed as an all-encompassing standard. Some of Suburbias more cynical critics could cite this stereotyping of the home as akin to moral and social propaganda; It is what you are born in, it is what you will live in, it is what you will die in.

'The material home represents the concrete expression of saving for a home of your own. Your advanced socialist may rage against private property even whilst he acquires it, but one of the best instincts in us is that which induces us to have one little piece of earth with a house and a garden which is ours. My home is where my wife and children are. The instinct to be with them is the instinct of a civilised man.'
Sir Robert Menzies, Ex. Australian Prime Minister.[1]

'It is remarkable how many case studies have been completed without a serious engagement with the oral history of suburbanites. In fact the evidence of most suburban studies ignores the testimony of suburbanites themselves and instead concentrates on the published perceptions of urban planners, architects and politicians whose careers are invariably dominated by urban issues. Suburbia has become a critical target understood through aerial photography. It is understood as a scenario instead of a real world.'[2]

Generics   Since the post-war explosion of Suburban form in Europe & America, there has been much academic writing and analysis on the subject of suburban housing and on the society it has created. Most of this writing subscribes to at least one of these two generic critiques.

Generic Suburban Critique No. 1   The Suburban Format

The formal layout and planning of generic suburban housing areas has often been referred to as network architecture; A network of static housing units which combine to produce assembled living areas that more resemble electronic circuit boards than residential areas; The suburban tract house.

Lewis Mumford, defines the 'Archetypal Suburban Form' in his 1961 publication 'The City in History'; 'Multitude of uniform, unidentifiable houses, lined up inflexibility, uniform distances, uniform roads, treeless communal wasteground, people of the same class, people of the same income, People of the same age group, witnessing the same television performances, eating the same prefabricated foods from the same freezers, conforming in every outward and inward respect to a common mould.' The suburban format, consists of both an architectural and social protocol.

The manicured housing estate; Socially, Suburbia is in its purest form a world of predominantly Middle-Class where people are seen as 'Smug, homogenised, self-indulgent, and indifferent to the destructive impact on the city'[1]. When all housing is constructed to a similar format, aspiration and personal differentiation can often manifest itself through the act of acquiring, consuming and competitive spending. Instead of achieving a proposed 'unified virtual village', a newly built area can quickly evolve into a plantation of those whose common ground repels through material competition rather than bring together. Suburban housing itself now acts as a social sieve whilst postal codes become labels of status. This artificial village is confounded by an aesthetic sameness. This artificiality is only reaffirmed by the commercial residues of moral ideologies, ie. A system of standardised religion and processed family mindedness which blurs an already superficial structure of generic moral and social codes.

Generic Suburban Critique No. 2   The Commercial Rhetoric of
The Good life (™) 'I live in a lovely quite residential area.'

The Good Life(™) represents the commercial bastardisation of a basic ideology that implies home ownership as the bastion of society. It is this commercial mythology which takes wholesome family values and neighbourliness as standard. The Good Life romance finds its roots in the rural ideology of escapism and differentiation from a chaotic city centre. The romantic suburb represents a meeting point between nature and commerce. As a result, the rhetoric of family and domesticity plays an important role in today's commercial world. 'Healthy, wealthy and wise'. Domesticity meets international, capitalist modernization. The 'house' has become the customers' prescribed home/castle with the relevant housing estate as his prescribed kingdom. The designs of the majority of housing schemes in Suburbia are dominated by the constraints of traditional family mindedness, ignorant of all other social structures of habitation eg, single parents, childless couples, retired workers... etc. Each house on average consists of One Kitchen, One Livingroom, Two Bathrooms (one up one down), Three Bedrooms (one for parents, two for children), Front Garden and driveway (Big Red Shiny car), Back Garden (Barbecue) and Garden Shed (barbecue storage).™

Notes
1 & 2 'Suburban Discipline'
P. Lang & T. Miller, Princeton Architectural Press, 1997.

Bibliography
'Contact & Controle'
Wies van Moorsel, SUA, Amsterdam, 1992.

'Saving the City, How to Halt the Destruction of Dublin'
Frank Mc Donald, Tomar Publishing, 1990.

'Dublin Crisis Conference Report'
Frank Mc Donald, Planning Seminar 1990.

'Planning, The Irish Experience'
Michael J. Bannon, Wolfhound Press, 1987.

'Good City Form'
Kevin Lynch, MIT Press 1981.

'Suburban Growth'
James H. Johnson, J. Wiley & Sons, 1975.

'Learning from Las Vegas'
Robert Venturi, MIT Press, 1972.

'The Death & Life of Great American Cities'
Jane Jacobs, Pelican, 1972.

'Los Angeles, The Architecture of Four Ecologies'
Reyner Banham, Penguin, 1971.

'The City in History'
Lewis Mumford, Penguin, 1961.

'Dreaming the Rational City'
M. Christine Boyer.

'Public Planning in the Netherlands'
A. K. Dutt & F. J. Costa.

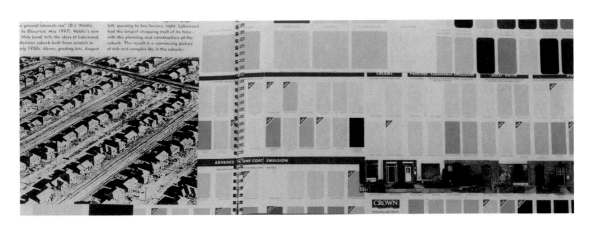

ground interests me" (D.J. Waldie, to Blueprint, May 1997). Waldie's new Holy Land, tells the story of Lakewood, fornian suburb built from scratch in early 1950s. Above, grading lots, August

left, queuing to buy houses, right, Lakewood had the largest shopping mall of its time – with the planning and construction of the suburb. The result is a convincing picture of rich and complex life in the suburbs.

GO WEST

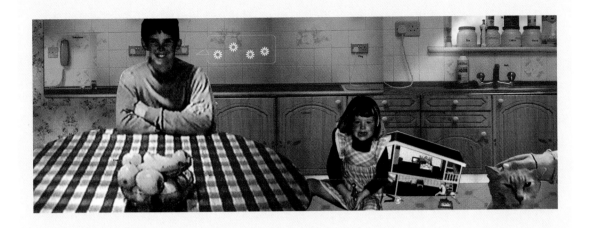

PAULINE TERREEHORST

Normality

ALEXANDRA LANG

& Legibility

FLOOR HOUBEN

A Walk through the City We leave our house and set out. It seems so simple, but how do we really move forward? What determine the signals or brain-storms on which we base our choices to go left or to go right, to take one route and not the other? How do we relate to the other people we come across?

These are questions that the hermit in the forest may be less likely to ask himself, although he or she will have daily routines to mark his environment as he steps over the fallen tree, past the river and the rabbit hole. Those who live in the city know themselves to be a perpetual part of a system of messages, of symbols. Anonymous passers-by evaluate one another on the basis of external characteristics. People find their way according to a man-made environment, and that environment is seldom neutral, the way the tree is virtually neutral. Every building, too, is strewn with signs that make it possible for us to classify it. Is it an office or a residence? Are the inhabitants – based on the curtains hanging in the windows – inventive or conservative people? And we have not even mentioned the actual signs meant to guide our behaviour: the more literal signs that direct or prohibit, indicating who may and may not use which path – so the pedestrian does not inadvertently find himself stranded on a superhighway.

Making judgements and finding our way are activities that can be directed. Often, signs are not even required. A number of people dress intentionally according to a certain norm, making themselves a sign of something, and they are assured an appropriate reaction. The businessman in a good three-piece suit and the young father on rollerblades will certainly notice the difference when they stand before a bank teller. The man-made environment is just as forceful in directing behaviour. A business neighbourhood does not encourage street parties, while a park invites people to wander aimlessly, enjoying their surroundings.

Not everyone seems to view this system of signs and signals as a constraint, as a restricting corset from which they really must escape. 'City air is liberating.' It is the far less 'besignalled' and signposted countryside that is experienced as the place that is not free. The framework of the city even appears capable of offering freedom in the regularity of its many parts. To disappear in the anonymity, not be recognized, loose yourself in arranged patterns, is a wish that can easily be fulfilled in the city, where so many buildings look alike, where so much is geared to the masses and not to the individual.

Floor Houben and Alexandra Lang have both conducted investigations of the signs and signals found in public spaces in cities – but their conclusions are diametrically opposed! Alexandra Lang took the 'do-and-don't-do' signs and public advertisements that direct our behaviour as her starting point. She replaces their messages with incentives not to comply with the norm. Floor Houben, in contrast, sooner emphasizes the orderly support that people actually seek out in the city in the form of repetition, a framework, or a pattern that a recognizable, familiar environment provides.

Of the two, Alexandra Lang reacts most strongly to her environment. In almost every visual signal designed to influence our behaviour, she recognizes an authority that would mould us to an ideal: the obedient citizen, the well-heeled, healthy, reasonable consumer, the perfect man and woman. As have many designers before her (Holzer, Kruger, Wool, Wiener), she attempts to unmask that authority. She shares their concern about public space being filled up by texts that order us about, always showing us the way. She does not interpret that concern in what would be at least as constraining a warning as has sometimes been the case in the course of the history of design. Instead, she combines the two dominant systems of signs in public space – traffic signs and advertising placards. The combination leads to an ironic commentary on both. Her 'traffic signs' impel us to pause at the text, take a moment to concentrate on the content. What, in fact, does 'a completely new sense of colour' actually mean? Or, 'One cannot have everything they want in life. Why not?' Why not, indeed.

By way of the texts and that ensuing moment of reflection, Lang's work focuses on allowing those who use public space to relax – for once, they needn't do a thing. She wants to create 'chilling-out' spaces. At the same time – and this is a part of her work which she does not make a problem of – her work continues to alert people to conscious activity. A passer-by, a participant in human social traffic, is also urged forward, to stop and think, for once, about the texts he is presented with. No sanction follows, the way another kind of sanction can result from ignoring a traffic sign. Equally, there is no sanction for refusing to adapt to the dominant ideal. Another kind of sanction is perhaps conceivable: that of intellectual exclusion, banishment to the land of the ignorant, of those who do not think about the images or texts that surround them. Those who join in with the traffic in Lang's park will find it difficult to avoid its rather compelling signs. They are forced to respond.

Carefully and meticulously, Lang has investigated a small, problematic terrain. Herein lies her strength. But 'her' public space is filled with a system of signs, a system that the visually literate, now accustomed to the double entendres that today's advertising also makes use of. Alexandra Lang's traffic signs offer an alternative to this sport, a brief, lucid insight into what it all should be about, a slightly alienating effect in an existence with a repetitiveness of which we are happily not always fully aware. Being able to pull back from that regularity, not having to watch out and therefore refusing to play along with the game can be an interesting position. But Lang does not accept that. She keeps us on the alert.

We leave our front door and go for a walk. What then do we do, what do we see? According to Floor Houben, we make use of fixed patterns. We adopt laws of order, arranging ourselves according to patterns reminiscent of Chomsky's innate ideas – whose grammatical framework was established long before the child began colouring it in with his own personal vocabulary. Floor Houben observes human behaviour. She unveils the identical signals that different people use: scores of windows with the same curtains, dozens of front doors with the same automobiles parked out front, dozens of identically-clad Moslem women populating our picture of the street, and dozens of patches of grass, garden fences that seem copies of one another. Floor Houben is concerned with that order which architects also employ in their work, with the need for harmony to stave off chaos. Every human being orders his or her environment. Anyone failing to do so for an extended period of time is ripe for institutional confinement. With this yearning for a light, pleasing, unencumbered order, Houben plays a surprising game. She does two things. She classifies and disorientates.

Floor Houben does not pass judgement, but seems simply to be in a state of wonderment about the diverse signs of order, the curtains, the lawns, the fences that mark the passage from the public to the private domain. She shows them off in a new way. The window with the Fiberglas curtains as a poster, the hedgerow as a design for panty hose – that lead that way to the most intimate of private domains. Everything and everyone is equally capable of changing into a product, even a billboard, as the prostitute in her flesh-coloured dress all too obviously demonstrates. Even the trash bag provides a place for advertising, and the neighbourhood watch fits on a poster. Images of the ideal family can be cast in rubber, but do equally good service as a print on a pair of white socks – the favourite colour of the average man. Our craving for uniformity reveals itself in such details. Houben herself goes farthest in this inclination to order, arranging nail clippings and squashed mosquitoes so that they produce a wallpaper design or an unusual bathroom tile. She is indefatigable in applying her ideas to every imaginable location. She adds a new layer to the apparent neutrality of this arranging of our affairs, so that order no longer looks so simple, insignificant and neutral. It becomes special, amusing – but never oppressive. Here, the ironic step back is not coloured by aversion, but by an acceptance and a conciliation with all-too-familiar human behaviour – and the deficiency that is always demonstrated by our choice for anonymity. Not everyone is tolerant to the exception.

The work of Alexandra Lang and Floor Houben reveals how public space is occupied by private symbols – applied consciously by themselves or by others to influence or guide individual behaviour. Choosing to study this image is at the moment all the more remarkable as there is now wide-scale debate about public space. Public space is more and more in the hands of private parties, such as shopping centres – in the legal sense as well. Cameras watch over public roads, sometimes twenty-four hours a day, so that diversions from the norm can immediately be responded to. The normalization to which both Lang and Houben refer makes public space even more orderly, more comprehensible than it already was. But appearances deceive, in just the same way that the – well-adapted – behaviour of each and every passing pedestrian deceives. Seemingly in a kind of dream state, he takes a walk, but in fact he is playing his role in the larger game of signs and signals that surrounds him. He is an actor performing in a décor. That awareness is always present. He uses every moment of that décor as the backdrop for dreams of his own. A living room with (fake) lace curtains can be the setting for a science fiction epic. The by-passer adjusts the décor according to his own personal needs, just the way he turns on or off whatever it is he wants or does not want to see on his television screen. His imagination is boundless. But there is no one watching.

Normality

ALEXANDRA LANG

& Legebility

FLOOR HOUBEN

Chill-out places My choice fell on the topic 'Man in public' as the general public is controlled to a large degree. Public spaces incapacitate, isolate and influence people externally. Due to the forces in public spaces, people see themselves far less as individuals and start to define and see themselves not through the characteristics inherent in their own personality but through other, that is to say external characteristics. This can above all be seen in advertising in public, which always promises the consumer that by using a certain product they will become a certain type of person with very particular characteristics worth striving for, thus corresponding to a certain ideal which constantly changes. Advertising makes promises it cannot keep. For example, the manufacturers of brand articles advertise by giving the buyers of their products a distinctiveness and thus a personal identity. However, in reality the buyer of such products belongs to a target group, that is to say they are one of a number of 'like-mined' people. Individuals feel the need to be part of a group. Advertising makes use of this and the consumer finds it very difficult to escape. These forces do not make it easy for the individual to find himself. It is easier to escape from such forces when one is in harmony with oneself. Man should first find his own, unique identity. These forces become clear in public as well, especially in traffic in signposting.

We all know situations very well, in which external forces influence everything we do. We observe certain laws, not least because we know that violations are punished. At school, at work, in short in every form of human co-existence, rules and standards prevail which fundamentally influence our behaviour. External forces can be weak or strong; we can see them as justified or arbitrary; in any case we know that they restrict our scope of action. We cannot do as we please on the world. However at least we feel as if we are lord and master in our own homes, that is to say at home. We see the thoughts that we think as our own. Our feelings can be pleasant or painful, but they're ours. But above all we are convinced that we can do what we like, within limits of course which are imposed by the external forces.

It will be my task to provide people in every day life with chill-out places in public, by placing certain signs to produce positive responses in the observer in the controlled public space, to urge him to think about himself and to communicate directly. This will be done with texts placed in public spaces, which relate to certain familiar situations.

In almost every visual signal designed to influence our behaviour, there is an authority that would mould us to an idea.

PAULINE TERREEHORST

12. Worauf weist dieses Verkehrszeichen hin?

☐ Erlaube ich es Ihnen, mich anzumachen?

☐ Weshalb wollen Sie mich anmachen?

☐ Für wie lange wollen Sie mich anmachen?

30
SIE KÖNNEN MICH
ANMACHEN...

13. Durch welche Fahrzeuge können bei Mißachtung dieses Verkehrszeichen schwere Unfälle entstehen?

☐ Schaue ich hin oder schaue ich weg?

☐ Warum schaue ich weg?

☐ Schaue ich bewußt weg?

◀ Schau mich an ▶

14. In welchem Fall müssen Sie vor diesem Verkehrszeichen warten?

☐ Habe ich ein Ziel?

☐ Wollen sie über Ihre Ziele sprechen?

☐ Braucht man Ziele im Leben?

15. In welche Richtungen dürfen Sie weiterfahren?

☐ Bin ich ausgeglichen?

☐ Tue ich etwas dafür, um ausgeglichen zu sein?

☐ Können sie sich Ihre innere Unruhe erklären?

Wer ausgeglichen ist, hat
einfach mehr vom Leben.

The following pages show a selection of traffic signs and public notices, which in my opinion are extremely discouraging and alienating.

In Germany today, the landscape of traffic signs includes four categories of signs

1. Regulatory Signs – Prohibitions

No Stopping

2. Regulatory Signs – Commands

Snow Chains Required

I have categorized the world of signs, posters and billboards in Germany today into ten categories.
Examples of four of these categories are included here, subdivided into respective types of signs.

Creating a Mood

Moralistic Text

Making only small mistakes is a good thing.
Learning from those mistakes is better.

3. Warning Signs

Baustelle

4. Instructional Signs

Parking for Authorized Persons Only

Ambiguity

The Query

In order to create the resting places – 'chill-out' places – I am aiming for, it seems sensible to replace forceful elements in traffic signs with promotional texts, aimed at the public and easy to interpret.

"Stark ist, wer keine Fehler macht. Stärker, wer aus seinen Fehlern lernt."

=

+

–

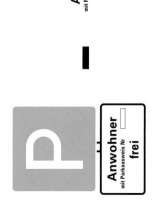

This is a location for a traffic exercise that reflects reality in the form of a model. The traffic circle serves as an example for building a model that demonstrates the price we pay for signs in public spaces. The model also makes it clear how sign texts impose on and interfere with one another.

OPPOSITIONS
PAULINE TERREEHORST
Normality
ALEXANDRA LANG
& Legebility
FLOOR HOUBEN

Products of Behaviour   (1999)

They are on offer in a promotional brochure, but they only exist on paper. Still, these 'products of behaviour' could simply be produced. Houben's diverse products are a kind of commercial 'ready-mades'. They are answers to the considerable need for variety in our daily consumption, a need evolved from the longing to distinguish ourselves from others. This yearning, paradoxically enough, goes hand in hand with our herding instincts, which explains why we seek that distinction in (the repetition of) forms that we share with others.

The external appearance of a product says something about the behaviour of its users. In this way, products also represent human need for security, control and recognition. These are three basic requirements that strongly determine how our environment is put together. In order to couple this onto something 'sellable', you have to touch a receptive chord in the buyer. Visual motifs lend themselves perfectly to this, because the surface appearance of a product can serve as a vehicle and point of recognition. By viewing the environment we live in as a product, it becomes possible to divide that environment into a 'samples palette'. Every sample or visual motif is a direct reflection of reality, and is therefore recognizable for the potential buyer of a product. The cross-fertilization between behaviour and product offers endless variations within the boundaries it has itself created. In Products of Behaviour, everyone will find something to suit his or her own taste.

Every human being orders his or her environment. Anyone failing to do so for an extended period of time is ripe for institutional confinement.

PAULINE TERREEHORST

Productenvan Gedrag

Products of Behaviour

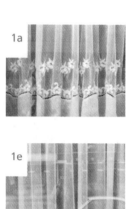

1a

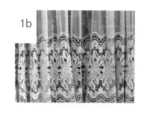

1b

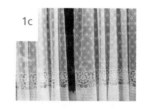

1c

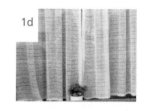

1d

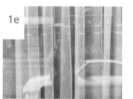

1e

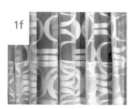

1f

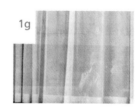

1g

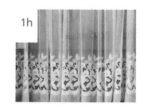

1h

2

3

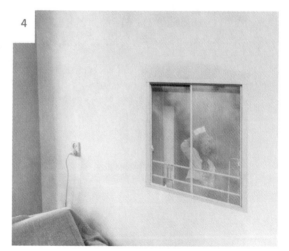

4

1A-5B TERRITORY/*A predictable, stable environment where the individual moves between continually repeated elements*

    1a-1h Samples/*Reality*

    2 House/*Territory*

    3 Window/*View*

    4 Poster/*Snoop Culture*

    5a Action/*Neighbourly Window Event: Spangen*

    5b Poster/*Friendly Window*

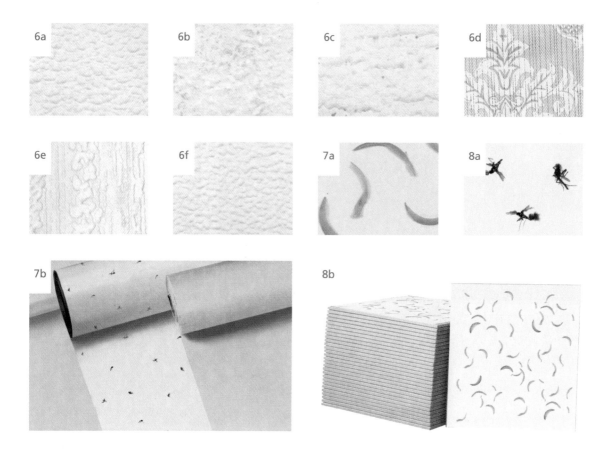

6a

6b

6c

6d

6e

6f

7a

8a

7b

8b

8c

6A-8C CONTROL/*Correcting the body and the environment*

    6a-6f Samples/*Reality*

    7a-7b Wallpaper/*Squashed Mosquitoes*

    8a-8c Tiles/*Nail clippings*

13a

13b

13c

Liguster

Conifeer

9A-13C SAFETY/*Restraining nature, creating territories*

    9a-9h Samples/*Reality*

    10 Auto/*Hedgeprint*

    11 Flat/*Green Experience*

    12 Poster/*Park Green*

    13a-13c Panty/*Hedgeprint*

14a

14b

14c

14d

14e

14f

14g

14h

15a

16

15b

ProductenvanGedrag

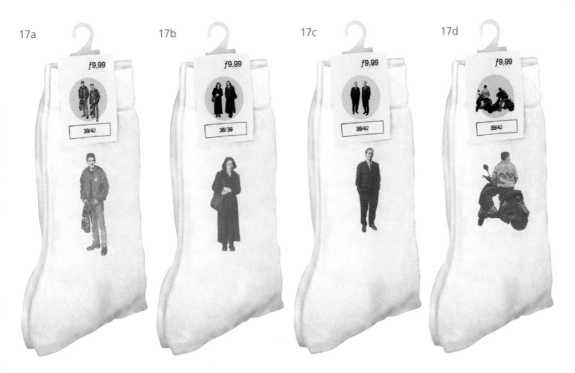

17a ƒ9,99 39/42

17b ƒ9,99 36/39

17c ƒ9,99 39/42

17d ƒ9,99 39/42

14A-17D RECOGNITION/*Reflecting and directing the environment*

      14a-14h Samples/*Reality*

      15a-15b Trees/*Public Space*

      16 Statuettes/*Muslim*

      17a-17d Socks/*Pairs*

COPY©PROOF
A New Method for
Design and Education
Who's who at Post-St. Joost

Director

Jules van de Vijver

Staff

Edith Gruson

Hugues C. Boekraad

Gerard Hadders

Marten Jongema

Simon Davies

Wouter Vanstiphout

Geert Setola (through June, 1996)

External Jury Members

Marie Helène Cornips

 *director of art and design, KPN
 Nederland*

Frans de la Haye

 industrial designer

Joke Robaard

 photographer, visual artist

Contributors to previous publications

Linda Roodenburg

 *former policy staff member,
 Photography Institute; independent consultant for photography
 projects*

Herman Beck

 *professor of Phenomenology
 of Religions at the Department
 of Theology, University of Tilburg*

Karin Spaink

 *writer, essayist on new media /
 cyberspace, Amsterdam*

Rob Kroes

 *professor of Americanology,
 University of Amsterdam*

Max Bruinsma

 *journalist, former Editor in Chief,
 Eye Magazine, London*

Visiting Lecturers

Evert van Ginkel

 archeologist

Cor van de Lugt

 forensic researcher

Ruud Moerkerken

 *spokesperson Corporate Identity
 TNT Benelux*

Len de Klerk

 *urban demographer, city of
 Rotterdam*

Wim van Es

 *advisor on urban development
 and planning*

Klaas jan Hindriks

 journalist, media trainer

Piet de Jonge

 *curator, Boymans van Beuningen
 Museum*

Wim Pijbes

 *assistant director, Kunsthal
 Rotterdam*

Willem Oomens

 *policy staff member for cultural
 affairs, city of Breda*

Cassandra Wilkins

 architectural historian

Ineke Smits

 film director

Arthur Japin

 novel and scenario writer

Wim Franssen

 film historian

Ronald Lagendijk

 copy writer

Jeroen Linssen

 philosopher

Karel van der Waarde

 *graphic designer, information
 graphics designer*

Frans Godfroy

 journalist

Prof. Bijlert

 historian: Modern India

Prof. Gommans

 historian: Ancient India

Jogi Panghaal

 industrial designer, New Delhi

Edwin Walvisch

 photographer

Hans Werleman

 photographer

Linda Roodenburg

 *former policy staff member,
 Photography Institute; independent consultant for photography
 projects*

Wanda Reiff

 gallery owner/director

Jan Eijkelboom

 *writer, poet, translator of English
 poetry*

Wiel Kusters

 *professor of literature, University
 of Maastricht*

Meghan Ferril

 *project director, Poetry in the
 Stedelijk Museum Amsterdam*

Bert Jansen
  journalist for arts & culture,
  NRC Handelsblad, Amsterdam
Wigger Bierma
  graphic designer, director,
  Typografische Werkplaats,
  Arnhem
Karel Martens
  graphic designer, director,
  Typografische Werkplaats,
  Arnhem
Anette Lenz
  graphic designer, Paris
Berry van Gerwen
  graphic designer
Carel Kuitenbrouwer
  journalist, design critic
Rob Schröder
  graphic designer, director
  Sandberg Institute, Amsterdam
Max Kisman
  graphic designer
Lucas Verwey
  urban planner
Joke Robaard
  photographer, visual artist
Paul Donker Duyvis
  visual artist
Geert van der Camp
  visual artist
Suleyman Dönmez
  Turkish community relations
  advisor, city of Rotterdam
Ahmed Mokhtari
  Morrocan community relations
  advisor, city of Rotterdam

Irma Boom
  graphic designer
Linda van Deursen
  graphic designer
Armand Mevis
  graphic designer

Department assistant
Nancy Stipkovits

Students (1995-2000)
Judith Boon
Charles Crimmins
Heike Czerner
Liesbeth Dierick
Barbara Dijkhuis
Stijn Druyts
Alan Fitzpatrick
Gerard Fox
Suzanne van Griensven
Rob Hazendonk
Joost van der Heijden
Tessa Hofland
Pauline Hoogweg
Floor Houben
Lieke Jonker
Mischa Keijser
Jeroen Klomp
Alexandra Lang
Ruth Leene
Heiko Liebel
Steffen Maas
Jantien Methorst
Jacek Mrowczyk
Niels van Ommeren
Sandra Oom
Jan Peeters

Jeroen Peetoom
Sheri Pressler
JanJaap Rypkema
Matthew Sanabria
Bianca Sistermans
Paul Snijder
Birgit Stuit
Ketherine Szeto
Andreas Tetzlaff
Minke Themans
Sanne Tulp
Marijn van Vilsteren
Daan Wormsbecher
Stef van Zimmeren
Peter Zuiderwijk

1st trimester

theory

the process of identification;
introduction to:
anthropology
sociology
psychology
semiology

exercise

forensic portrait;
self portrait
imaginary portrait

the identity of the designer
deconstruction of the design elements
image, text, colour
3 squares #1
found image, text, colour
3 squares #2
created image, text, colour
3 squares #3
hand-made image, text, colour

visitors

forensic detective
archeologist
corporate communication consultant
media trainer
museum curator

identities

2nd trimester

theory

history of architecture and
urban development;

city excursions:
historical (paris, new delhi)
modernist (nagele)
reconstructed (rotterdam)
postmodern (eurodisney, euralille)

exercise

index and meaning;
visual essay

visitors

the profession;
designers
architects
visual artists
photogaphers
film-makers

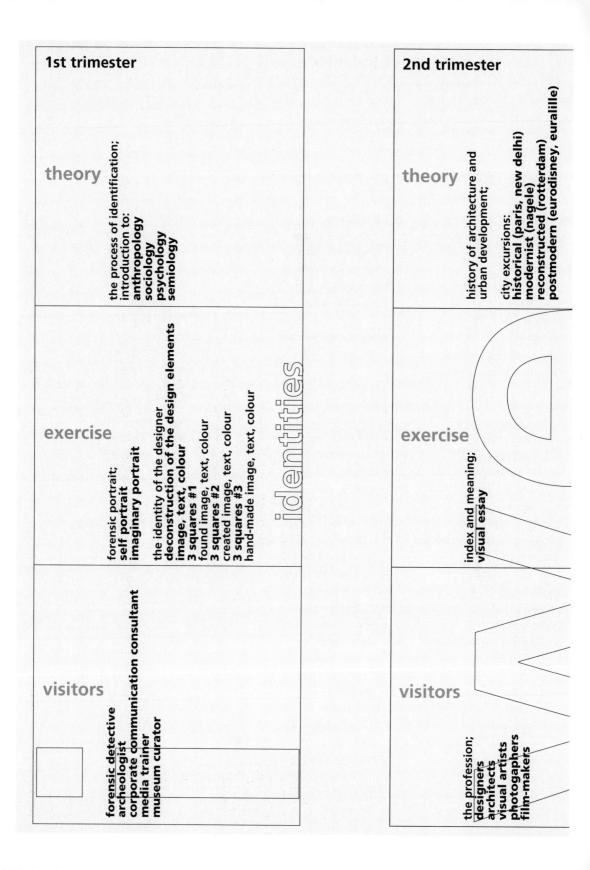

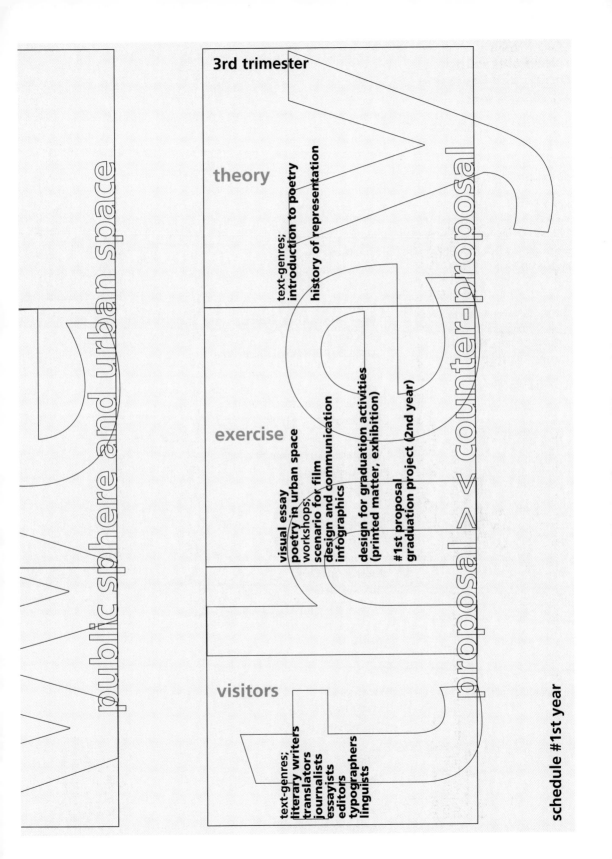

public sphere and urban space

3rd trimester

theory

text-genres;
introduction to poetry
history of representation

exercise

visual essay
poetry in urban space
workshops;
scenario for film
design and communication
infographics

design for graduation activities
(printed matter, exhibition)

#1st proposal
graduation project (2nd year)

proposal > counter-proposal

visitors

text-genres;
literary writers
translators
journalists
essayists
editors
typographers
linguists

schedule #1st year

COPY©PROOF
A New Method for
Design and Education
Acknowledgements

Copy Proof is a publication of Post-St. Joost, graduate programme of the St. Joost Academy, Hogeschool Brabant, Breda.

© 2000 St. Joost Academy, Breda
(www.stjoost.nl)/
010 Publishers, Rotterdam
(www.010publishers.nl)

ISBN 90 6450 398 2

Editorial Concept
Hugues C. Boekraad
Edith Gruson
Gerard Hadders
Gert Staal

Compilation and Final Editing
Edith Gruson
Staal & de Rijk/Editors, Amsterdam

Texts
Hugues C. Boekraad
Gert Staal

**Visual Essay on Complexity
in Reading Design**
Gerard Hadders

Essays
H.J.A Hofland
Martin Reints
Pauline Terreehorst
Dirk van Weelden
A.J.A. van Zoest

Translation
Mari Shields, Amsterdam

Photography
Mischa Keijser
Bas Wilders (a.o.)

Design
Pauline Hoogweg, Breda

Printing
Lecturis bv, Eindhoven